PYTHON
CRASH COURSE

The Complete Beginner's Guide to Learn Python Programming and Effectively Understand Faster Computer Programming (Learn Python Coding Language, Advanced, To Expert concepts)

ANTONIO ROBERT

ASIN: B07VXLD1CN

ISBN: 9781086920321

TABLE OF CONTENTS

Introduction

Python is a programming language developed by Guido Van rossum in Amsterdam in the early 90s. Contrary to what is supposed, the name does not come from the python snake, but from the show of the comedy troupe MonthyPython, which Rossum adored.

Python is an object-oriented, interpretive, modular, and interactive, high-level language. Programming languages are the bridge between machine logic and human logic. The fact that a word is closer to the machine logic results in the ability to work on the machine faster. However, approaching machine logic requires distancing from human reasoning and making the language more difficult to learn. If a programming language moves away from machine logic and approaches human logic, it is called a high-level python, so it is a high-level language. It is easier to learn than most languages.

With Python, you can accomplish many tasks you need with a small number of lines of code. You can quickly write many programs such as desktop applications, web applications, data analysis, and visualization applications with python.

Example from Java:

```
1  class merhaba
2  {
3  public static void main(String args[])
4  {
5  System.out.println("Merhaba Dünya!");
6  }
7  }
```

Python language with "Hello World":

```
1  print("Merhaba Dünya")
```

Also, the curly bracket ("{}"), which is used to identify blocks in python in many languages, is used by specifying the same blocks to identify blocks and by typing inward or outward lines to indicate hierarchy.

Why Would You Want to Learn Programming?

Take a look at your daily life. Whether you are at work or home, you will see that you uniformly repeat specific jobs. For example, you may be working in a post that requires you to deal with written documents always. Maybe you open dozens of reports every day, looking for information in these documents, correcting, renewing or deleting this information. Imagine how time-consuming and tedious these processes are. If you knew a programming language, you could have done all this for you.

This is where the Python programming language comes into play. You can complete your work every day for hours with the help of only a few lines of Python code.

Or think about it like this: You might be getting a lot of fun with PDF documents in the workplace. Maybe you need to convert hundreds of pages of stamped and signed papers into PDF. You may also be asked to PDF these documents in one piece as much as possible. But as he passes hundreds of pages through the scanner, something goes wrong in the middle, the machine malfunctions, and perhaps your document is inevitably split.

This is where the Python programming language comes into play. If you learn the Python programming language, instead of looking for hours of free PDF merge on the Internet, or giving tens of dollars to professional software, you can put together your documents and write the program to do your job.

Of course, what you can do with Python is not limited to the simple examples given above. Using Python, you can work in many areas such as desktop programming, game programming, portable device programming, web programming, and network programming.

PART I

Beginner's guide

One of the significant features of Python programs is that they can be run without the need to compile, unlike languages such as C and C ++. Since compiling is eliminated in Python, the program can be developed very quickly with this language.

In addition, the simple and clean syntax of the Python programming language has made it a preferred language for many programmers. Python's syntax is clean and simple, making it easy to write programs and read a program written by someone else.

Thanks to the features mentioned above of Python, large, globally renowned organizations (such as Google, YouTube, and Yahoo!) always need Python programmers within them. For example, many big companies provide job opportunities for Python-aware programmers, Python's chief developer Guido Van Rossum worked at Google between 2005 and 2012, and in late 2012, the transition to Dropbox company, the importance, and validity of this programming language is probably more it will appear prominently.

Why Python?

Python is an interpretive language, meaning it can be run without the need to compile, unlike languages such as C and C ++. This still makes it easier to develop programs with Python. Many things you need to write a program in Python, data structures, functions are already available to you. In this way, as in other languages to solve a problem without the need to design to the finest details you can write presentations with the infrastructure much more quickly program

Python has a simple syntax. This makes it easier and more enjoyable to write programs, as well as more easily understand the programs written by others. Python allows you to do much with little code.

What makes a programming language powerful is its ability to work on different platforms. Python can run on almost any platform. Windows, Linux, Unix, Mac, Symbian, and more...

The Python language is the center of many world-famous attractions with its advantages. Organizations such as Google, Youtube, Yahoo always need Python programmers.

Python Versions

Python has been developed since 1990. Python version 1.0 was released in January 1994. The Python 2 series follow this. Python series is also available in lower versions, such as 2.7.11. In general, these series are expressed with names such as 2.x, 3.x. There are currently a large number of programs on the market written in Python 2.x series.

Python 3 is a more robust, error-free, and more powerful language than Python 2. When creating Python 3, there have been major changes compared to Python 2.

At this point, there may be a question about which Python series to learn. If you are new to Python, it is of course a logical decision to learn Python 3. However, if you are going to work on a project written in Python, you will need to know the version in which the project was developed because all the modules that were in use before Python 3 have not been transferred to Python 3 yet. But over time the conversion will be completed and Python 3 will eliminate Python 2.

Python Installation

In order to develop programs with Python, you must have the corresponding version of Python installed on your computer. Many Linux distributions come with Python installed. Ubuntu comes with Python 2 and 3 installed. It is also installed on the Mac operating system. However, if you are using Windows, you must install Python yourself.

Where to use Python

Python is used in many areas, from engineering to finance. Since the 2000s, it has been widely used in scientific or computational studies. Both hardware and software developments have had ar impact on this:

In terms of hardware, processing power and memory (storage) capacity is quickly accessible and accessible to everyone, and in many cases, interpreted languages such as Python have become quite slow in some processes, and the use of high-level data structures can be neglected in many cases.

In terms of software, the widespread use of the Internet and the flow of open source or free software with it has brought the scientists who adopt this approach to work in coordination with the efficient tools developed on the Internet.

Python Scientific Computing Libraries

With Python, three main libraries are used for basic scientific computing: Numpy for some essential functions, such as fast array structures and matrix operations; SciPy is used for all tasks that may be needed for numerical integration, numerical integration, optimization and statistics, and Matplotlib library for two-dimensional and three-dimensional visualization at a certain level.

In addition to the above-mentioned libraries, there are advanced and stable standard library components for operations such as the manipulation of databases and Internet pages, which are frequently performed in scientific studies. In addition, comprehensive libraries have been developed specifically to particular disciplines, such as BioPython for biology.

```
1 ▾ def sum_of(F):
2 ▾     def do(A):
3           product = [F(a) for a in A]
4           return sum(product)
5
6       return do
7
8   sum_of_square = sum_of(lambda a: a**2)
9   sum_of_inverse = sum_of(lambda a: 1/a)
10
11  c = sum_of_square([1,2,3,4])
12  d = sum_of_inverse([1,2,3,4])
13
```

For specific areas of study, the reader can refer to sites such as SciPy for available libraries. In addition, there are practical interfaces for cal ing languages such as Fortran, C, R from Python that are widely used in scientific computing, link libraries for libraries such as the GNU scientific library, and various libraries for parallel calculations.

The development environment that can be used when making scientific calculations with Python is also very rich: First, of course, general (Python) development tools such as IDLE or Eclipse are available. For scientific developers, there are three different options that provide a more practical environment than MATLAB. Such environments have features such as explor variable explorer u, which is familiar to MATLAB users, and provides possibilities such as changing variables in place, and "object explorer", code analyzer "Pylint, ecek which can be very useful for new learners.

Sage5 or IPython (version> 0.12) can be used to obtain the notebook interface familiar to Mathematica or Maple users. (IPython is a standardized command-line Python environment developed specifically for scientific computing and used as standard. Many other projects (eg Spyder) provide rich interactive programming skills through Python.)

We have briefly mentioned above the use of Python in the field of scientific computing, which is widely accepted. In the remainder of the paper, we will try to show that Python is a good choice of programming languages for scientific computing training in almost all of our universities.

The Python programming language, which is free, was implemented in the standard version using the C language. With these codes, Python's standard library, development tools and many other libraries can be downloaded from the Internet as an open source free of charge and without any license issues. Therefore, all students in scientific computing classes will be able to use these tools freely wherever they want.

In addition, since Python's scientific libraries are open source, they will be able to examine the code of the modules they use for the topics covered in the course and adapt them to different purposes if necessary.

Easy to use Python is designed for easy learnability and use. This easy-to-learn feature is of course an important advantage for any use. In the context of scientific computation, if necessary, it is possible to teach the language to the students from the beginning in scientific computation classes and still give the possibility to devote time to the subjects that are intended to be studied. If students can take the programming courses before they come to their first course in scientific calculation, they will have the opportunity to study more subjects in more depth.

What is python?

Python's simplicity will make it easier to focus on the algorithms or scientific problems you want to learn. In addition, students will be able to read the code that they have written and others (especially my professors) more easily and will be able to assimilate the idea. Being interactive As a interpreted language, Python allows you to work interactively on the interpreter. There are three important benefits of this feature.

- The first is the ability to 'explore' quickly and interactively while learning new features of the language or new libraries.
- Second, it is easier to experiment quickly when writing a new program.
- The third benefit of scientific computing is that it helps to see the results of the calculations step by step and efficiently follow the formation of the problem at hand.

Supporting object-oriented programming the basic paradigms Python supports are procedural, object-oriented, and functional programming paradigms. It is a basic requirement to be able to work easily in the scientific calculation. In relatively large scientific software projects, it is preferable to use a language that supports object-oriented programming in terms of its convenience.

In addition, this paradigm provides a natural framework of work, especially in studies with physical purposes. Although it is not a standard method for determining the popularity of a programming language, measurements made by various approaches are almost identical and show that Python is one of the most popular languages.

In terms of the TIOBE site, Python is the sixth in the overall languages ranking; In the ranking of scripting languages, it is the second after PHP, the standard Internet. In addition, companies like Google have begun to use Python, allowing a large audience behind the language. Popularity is a programming language and has several rewards for its learners.

Width of the standard library developers emphasize that using the slogan için including batteries için for Python, the standard library can have tools for all kinds of work. This provides students with a consistent and portable framework for all their needs, both in their academic work and in other work.

Portability Programs written in Python, a compiled language, can run independently of the platform (of course, this requires the Python compiler and related libraries to be available on that computer). Therefore, it is possible to easily share programs between students and teachers without the need to create executable files in any way and adapt the program to different platforms.

Of course, it is not possible to argue that Python is advantageous in every respect. For example, this section does not mention points such as Python running much slower than compiled languages. In fact, this may be considered the only major disadvantage in terms of undergraduate scientific calculation. On the other hand, this speed difference, which is very grave in the worst case, is at a level that can be compensated by the absence of the compilation phase in the average case.

Today, when we think that human resources are more important than machine resources, Python seems to be the most appropriate language for scientific computing at the undergraduate level. "The most appropriate Burada is, of course, not elbette the best in every respect;; olmak being optimal. in all aspects. Lecturers at our universities can easily switch to Python in their classes by taking advantage of the freedom of free software and the wide range of rich teaching resources.

How to Run Python

In the previous section, we have explained in detail how to install Python on different platforms. In this section, we will see how to run this Python program on both GNU / Linux and Windows. First, let's see how GNU / Linux users can run Python.

GNU / Linux Users

As you can see in the previous chapters, we can install Python3 in different ways on GNU / Linux systems. In this section, we will examine how to run Python3 for each type of installation separately.

Installed Python3 Users

If you already have Python3 installed on your system, you can start Python3 by simply typing:

python

As of 20.10.2018, most GNU / Linux distributions have Python2 installed by default, so python when you run the command, the working version is probably Python2. Therefore, you python should pay attention to which version is installed by default and which version the command starts.

Both Python2 and Python3 may already be installed on your system. So you python3 can try to give the above command in the form of a.

For example, as of version 12.10 of the Ubuntu GNU / Linux distribution, the python command is Python2; python3is running Python3.

Builders of Python3 from Repository

The default version of Python in GNU / Linux distributions is predominantly Python2. Therefore, the pythoncommand runs versions of Python 2.x. Therefore, in order to avoid any conflict, GNU / Linux distributions try to name the Python3 package in a different way. The overwhelming majority of distributions currently on the market call the Python3 package 'python3'. Therefore, GNU / Linux users can start Python3 on the command line if they have installed Python using the package managers:

python3

You should then see a screen like this:

yazbel @ ubuntu: ~ $ # python3 [GCC 4.4.7 20120313 (Red Hat 4.4.7-3)] on linux Type "help", "copyright "," Credits "or" license "for more information. >>>

If you have seen the above screen, you are ready to program with Python. If not, you can go back and try to find out where things went wrong.

Here are a few tips on where things might have gone wrong:

When installing Python3, make sure that your package manager does not give any errors, so the program is installed successfully on your system. To do this, you can check if Python3 appears in the list of installed packages.

python3command is correct. One of the most common mistakes made especially by beginners in Python programming language is to misspell the word python. You may have accidentally typed python, pyton, or phyton instead of python, also python3note that the command consists entirely of lowercase letters. Python and python are not the same things from a computer standpoint.

The deployment policy of the distribution you are using may be different from the one described above. So the distribution you're using might have named the Python3 package differently. If this is the case, you can try to learn how to run Python3 using your distribution's help resources (wiki, forum, irc, help documentation, user lists, etc.) or by asking at forum.yazbel.com.

Let's come to the case of those who have compiled Python3 from the source...

Compilers of Python3 as root

If you compile Python3 with root rights from the source as described in the previous sections, the python3command will not work. You'll need to use the following command instead:

python3.7

Let's assume that the Python3 version you have installed is 3.7 . If you have installed a different version of Python3, you will of course need to use the name of that version as the launcher command. For example: python3.0or python3.1. In the meantime, python3.7there is a dot between the numbers of the number 37 command.

Just as in the installation from the package repository, if the above command does not allow you to run Python, something might have gone wrong during installation. For example, you may have received an error at any stage of the installation from the source, which may have prevented Python from installing.

As you can see, those who compile Python from the source specify the full version name of Python to run the Python programming language. You can continue to work in this way. You don't mind that. For your convenience, however, It's recommended that you place a symbolic link named py3 under / usr / bin / . So you can start Python3 just by giving the command.py3

So how do we do that?

Python is compiled from the source executable file in / usr / local / bin / directory in Python 3.7 (or, depending on the version you have installed python3 python3.0 or Python3.1) copied the name, therefore we python3.7need to use the command to run Python3. In order to run Python3, for example py3, if we just want to use a command like this, all we need to do is create a symbolic link named py3 under / usr / bin to the file named python 3.7 in / usr / local / bin / . For this we will use the command:ln

ln -s /usr/local/bin/python3.7 / usr / bin / py3

Of course, this command as an authorized user should not say I need to say. After issuing this command, you can now py3start the Python programming language with just the command.

A Very Important Warning

As we explained in the previous step, you downloaded Python3 from its official site and compiled it yourself. Pretty good. But at this point, there is the need to draw your attention to a very important issue. As said from the beginning, the Python programming language has a very important place in GNU / Linux operating systems. This programming language can be the backbone of the distribution you use.

For example, in Ubuntu GNU / Linux distribution, many system tools are written in Python. Therefore, pythonit is very important what the default Python version is on the system, and therefore which Python version the command runs. Because some vital tools on your system pythondepend on the version of Python that the command runs. Therefore, you pythonshould not touch the version of Python that this command runs.

For example, if you pythonare running one of the 2.x versions of Python on your operating system , do pythonnot link the command to another version of Python through symbolic links or other tools . In this way, you make the whole system unusable. Of course, if you have tried to install Python3 with the command, as described in the installation process, you can delete the link file you created later and link the command to the default version on the system. That way, everything goes back to the way it was. But if you have lost the files of the default Python version on your system because you installed Python with the command, there is not much to do for you... You will shed blood, sweat and tears to restore the system back to its stable state.make installmake altinstallpythonmake install

Likewise, python3it is also important whether the command in your deployment starts a specific version of Python by default. What pythonwe said about the command above python3and other similar commands are the same.

For example, in Ubuntu GNU / Linux distribution, the pythoncommand is Python 2.x, which is installed on the system; python3Since the command runs Python 3.x installed on the system, we have chosen names for the versions of Python that we have installed that will not conflict with the versions on the system, for example, to run our own version of Python3, we py3prefer a command like.

As a good test, you can thoroughly examine the output of the following command before you compile the Python programming language yourself:

ls -g {, / usr {, / local}} / bin | grep python

On systems with two versions of Python installed, this command will output something similar (the output is clipped):

dh_python2

dh_python3

pdb2.7 -> ../lib/python2.7/pdb.py

pdb3.7 -> ../lib/python3.7/pdb.py

py3versions -> ../share/python3/py3versions.py

python -> python 2.7

python2 -> python 2.7

python2.7

python3 -> python 3.7

python3.7 -> python3.7mu

the python3.7m

python3mu -> python3.7mu

pyversions -> ../share/python/pyversions.py

Pay attention to the parts we show in italics. As you can see, python and the python2commands are running Pythor version 2.7 on this system. python3 The command is the 3.7 version of Python.

In essence, as a GNU / Linux user, you should not delete any default Python versions on the system, nor modify any commands that reach the default version. If, for example, your system is python3already running a Python version, use another command name that does not conflict with the default name to reach your newly installed version of Python. So, for example, if the python3command is running version 3.7 of Python, create py3a symbolic link, such as to run your newly installed version. Let the default command (python, python3etc.) continue to run the default version of Python.

Never forget. As a programmer candidate, you are required to familiarize yourself with the operating system in which you will write the program. Therefore, you should know the behaviors that will make your operating system unstable, avoid these behaviors, and know how to get back if you do something wrong especially if you decide to compile a program from source...

Since we have made this serious warning, we can continue our journey with peace of mind.

Builders of Python3 in Home Directory

If you compile Python3 with limited user rights and instal it in your home directory, the above commands will not allow you to run Python. In order to run Python3, users who have already installed Python3 in their home directory will first access the directory where they installed Python3 from there, and then to the bin / folder under that directory and issue the following command:

./python3.7

Let's say you have installed Python3 in the directory $ HOME / python. First we access the directory $ HOME / python / bin:

cd $ HOME / python / bin

Then we issue the following command:

./python3.7

Now you know what the. / mark on the command is for ...

Of course it's assumed that the Python version you installed here is 3.7. If you have installed a different version, you have to type the command above.

You can continue working this way if you want. However, each time you come to the directory where Python is installed, running the command ./python3.7 there will turn into torment after a while. To make things easier, you should follow these steps:

1. Open the .profile (or .bash_profile or .bashrc) file under your home directory .

2. At the very end of this file, add a directory to the path that contains the file that allows us to run Python by placing a line like this:

export PATH = $ PATH: $ HOME / python / bin /

3. The $ HOME / python / bin / line indicates the directory under which the executable file for Python3 is located. Here I assume that the executable file of Python3 is in the $ HOME / python / bin directory. So I wrote a line like $ HOME / python / bin / . But if the executable file of Python3

is in a different directory, you should write this line accordingly.

4. After adding the appropriate line to your file, save and exit the file. To make our change to the file take effect, give the following command:

source .profile

Of course, if the name of the file on your system is .bash_profile or .bashrc , you should change the above command accordingly.

5. Then give a symbolic link to the file named $ HOME / python / bin / python 3.7 under $ HOME / python / bin / , for example, py3 :

ln -s $ HOME / python / bin / python3.7 $ HOME / python / bin / py3

6. Restart your computer.

7. Now you can start Python3, no matter where you are located by:

PC3

Here, too, if the above command does not allow you to run Python3, you may have done something missing or wrong. Visit forum.yazbel.com for assistance.

Assuming that you can successfully install and run Python3, let's move on.

Using Different Versions in GNU / Linux Together

As said before, there are currently two different Python series on the market: Python2 and Python3. Since it has been in use for a very long time, Python2 is more common than Python3. If you want to run programs written in Python2 and develop with Python3, you can choose to have both Python2 and Python3 on your system at the same time. So how do you do that?

As said in the beginning, Python2 is installed on almost all GNU / Linux distributions. So if you installed Python3 in addition to your system (from source or package repository), you don't need to do anything else. If you have followed the instructions described above, pythonPython2 will run when you issue the command in the console, and Python3 will run when you give the python3(or py3) command.

But if you don't even have Python2 installed, which is very unlikely, you can install Python2 on your system with the help of your package manager. There is very little GNU / Linux distribution currently on the market that does not have Python in the package repository.

Now that we've learned how to run Python on GNU / Linux and use different versions of Python together, we can look at the situation of Windows users.

Windows Users

Windows users can start Python3 in two ways:

Start> All Programs> Python 3.7 > Python 3.7.

pythonGiving the command on the command line.

If you choose the first path, you will have direct access to the command line that Python offers you. However, when you reach the Python command line in this way, you face some restrictions. Instead of directly accessing the Python command line, it is more logical to reach the MS-DOS command line first and then to the Python command line. So instead of reaching the command line this way, it's recommend you to choose the second option. To do so, access the command line and run the following command:

python

When you give this command, you will see a screen like this:

C: \ Users \ yazbel> python3 [MSC v.1600 32 bit (Intel)] on win32 Type "help", "copyright" , "Credits" or "license" for more information. >>>

If this command gives an error message instead of a screen similar to the above, you may have made some steps missing or incorrect during installation. If the above command doesn't work, you probably forgot to check the Add Python 3.7 to PATH box during installation. If so, you need to run the setup file again, perform the corresponding step, or add Python to the PATH yourself.

python Assuming that you can run the command successfully, let's continue.

Using Different Versions in Windows Together

As said before, there are currently two different Python series on the market: Python2 and Python3. Since it has been in use for a very long time, Python2 is more common than Python3. If you want to run programs written in Python2 and develop with Python3, you can choose to have both Python2 and Python3 on your system at the same time. So how do you do that?

It is very easy to do this in Windows. You can download different versions of Python on your computer by going to python.org/download and installing them normally on your computer. This way you can install as many different versions of Python as you want on your system. So how co you get these different versions?

Python offers us a special program called 'py' so that we can run different versions of Python on our computer.

The Py program is specific to Windows only. GNU / Linux does not have such a program.

To run the Py program, we get to the system command line and run the command:

py

When you give this command (theoretically), the last version of Python that you installed on your system wil start. However, this may not always be the case. Or your output may not be as you expect. So when you give this command, note which version starts.

If you have more than one version of Python installed on your system, you can start this version with the help of this script. For example, if you have both Python 2.x versions and Python 3.x installed, you can start Python 2.x with the following command:

py -2

To start Python 3.x, we issue the following command:

py -3

If you have more than one version of Python2 or more than one version of Python3 installed on your system, you can access the version you want by specifying the main and minor version numbers:

py -2.6

py -2.7

py -3.4

py -3.5

In the meantime, if you're careful, we have the ability to use pythonboth the pycommand to start Python programs. If you have a single version of Python installed on your system, pythonyou may want to use the command to start Python py;

Thus, we have acquired the most basic information about Python. Thanks to what we have learned in this section, we can install Python programming language on our computer and run this programming language successfully.

Which Command Runs Which Version?

Now we know how to install and run the Python programming language on our computer. However, because of the importance of the issue, there is a question that we want to emphasize again and make sure you know the answer: Which command, which version of Python s running on the operating system you are using?

By following the different methods described in this book, you may have installed the Python programming language on your computer in different ways. For example, if you installed the Python programming language through the package manager of the GNU / Linux distribution python3you are using, you may need to use the command to start Python. Likewise, if you installed Python on

Windows, pythonyou may be using the command to run this programming language. Unlike all this, if you downloaded and compiled Python's source code from your site, you might be using a different name to run Python. For example, perhaps py3you are using a command like Python to run...

Whichever command you use to run the Python programming language, please ask yourself the following questions before moving on to the next topic:

- Is the Python program already installed on my operating system?
- How many different Python versions are there in my operating system?
- python command does one of these Python versions run?
- python3 Does the command work?
- If so, which version of Python does it run?
- What command do I use to run the Python version I compiled from the source?

In this book we will assume:

- You are running the 2.x versions of Python with the pythoncommand on your operating system.
- You are running the 3.x versions of Python with the python3command on your operating system.

- When using this book, you should consider these assumptions, if you use different commands from them; you should set your code accordingly.

System Command Line and Python Command Line

So far we've got all the information on how to run the Python programming language. However, there is one common error that programming beginners often do: confuse the system command line with the Python command line.

Never forget that the command line of the operating system you are using and Python's command line are two different environments. So in Windows cmd, Ubuntu is Ctrl + Alt + T media that you get with, while the system command line, open this environment python3(or pythoneither py3) Python command-line environment that is dominated by the command. System system commands on the command line (eg cd, ls, dir, pwd) are given, the command-line Python, Python commands are given litt e later we start learning. Therefore, after you give the command python3(or pythonor py3), you will be frustrated if you try to use system commands such as and in the environment you reach .cd Desktopls

How to pronounce Python

Do we know how to pronounce python, a foreign word?

Although the developer is Dutch, python is an English word. Therefore, the rules of English are valid in the pronunciation of this word. However, it is not easy for native speakers to pronounce the word correctly. Because there is a [th] voice in this word which is not in Turkish and its pronunciation resembles peltek s. The english-speaking voice that thinks (think) will remember the words. Those whose native language is Turkish usually pronounce think as [tink]. So you can pronounce python as [paytın].

Some prefer to pronounce Python as a word [python]. Of course, you are free to choose a pronunciation in which your language is returned.

In the meantime, if you want to listen to the English pronunciation of python, you can visit howjsay.com, if you're wondering how Guido Van Rossum pronounces this word, you can watch the video at http://goo.gl/bx9iJu.

Platform Support

The Python programming language can run on many different operating systems and platforms. GNU / Linux, Windows, Mac OS X, AS / 400, BeOS, MorphOS, MS-DOS,

OS / 390, Z / OS, RiscOS, S60, Solaris, VMS, Windows CE, HP-UX, iOS and you can develop Python applications in many environments, such as Android, which you may not even have heard of. In addition, a Python program that you type in any environment can be run in other environments with no or minor modifications.

We will describe the Python programming language in GNU / Linux and Microsoft Windows operating system. But there is no special GNU / Linux distribution or Windows version to rely on. So no matter which GNU / Linux distribution or Windows version you're using, you can learn Python programming language and adapt what you've learned to your own operating system.

Because the author of these lines has access to computers running Ubuntu, CentOs, Windows 7, and Windows 10, the screenshots in this book will usually be taken from these operating systems.

How to Install Python?

In order to write programs with Python, this programming language must be installed on our computer. Whether you need to install this programming language depends on the operating system you are using. Here we will examine the status of both GNU / Linux and Windows users respectively and separately. Let's first look at the situation of GNU / Linux users:

Throughout this book, you will find that some topics are discussed separately for GNU / Linux and Windows users. However, even if the topics are separated in this way, I recommend that you read both because in these sections you will find information that might interest both user groups. You will also find that even though these sections address different user groups, they are actually complementary.

GNU / Linux Users

We need to consider some points when installing Python programming language on GNU / Linux distributions. In this section, we will examine what these important points are.

Installed Python Version

Almost all GNU / Linux distributions come with the Python programming language installed. For example, in Ubuntu, Python is already installed.

But here's the case:

As already mentioned, there are two different Python series currently on the market. You know one of them is Python's 2.x series and the other is the 3.x series.

To check the version of Python installed on your system, first try the following command on the command line (with a large 'V'):

python -V

If you get an output of Python 2.xy from this command, which starts with part 2 before x and y, Python2 is installed on your system.

However, the output of the command from Python 2.xy does not mean that only Python2 is installed on your system. Python2 and Python3 may already be installed on your system. For example, as of version 12.10 of Ubuntu GNU / Linux, both Python2 and Python3 are installed on the system.python -V

You can also try running the above command in order to check what the situation is in the GNU / Linux distribution you are using. If this command gives you a version number instead of an error message, Python3 is installed on your system.python3 -V

For a more accurate report of Python versions on your system, you can use the following command:

ls -g {, / usr {, / local}} / bin | grep python

You can also see if you have more than one version of Python installed on your system.

You can also obtain information about the versions of Python installed on your system by issuing a command such as the GNU / Linux distribution you are using. If you have Python3 installed on your system and you are satisfied with the installed version of Python3, you don't need to do anything. You can move on without trying to install a different version of Python.

Installation from Package Repository

There are two ways that GNU / Linux users who do not have any Python3 version installed by default on their systems, or who are not satisfied with the default Python3 version installed on their system, may prefer to get Python3: Even if Python3 is not installed on your system, this version may still be packaged in your distribution repositories. So it's suggested you open your package manager in accordance with your system and do a search using the word 'python' there. For example, there is Python3 in the package repositories of the Ubuntu GNU / Linux distribution. Therefore, Ubuntu users can install this package via the Ubuntu Software Center or directly with the following command, if it is not already installed on their system (which is probably installed):

Sudo apt-get install python3

This command will install Python3 on your computer with all its dependencies.

Installation from Source

What if you don't have Python3 in the repository of the distribution you're using, or if the version of Python3 in the repository is outdated and you want to use a newer version of Python3?

If you cannot find the Python3 package in the repositories of your distribution, or if the version in the repository does not satisfy you, you will need to compile Python3 from the source. When compiling Python3 from the source, you have two options: Install Python3 with root rights or install Python3 as an unauthorized user. Under normal circumstances, it's recommended that you install Python3 as an authorized user if you have root rights on the system you are using.

Installation with Root Rights

There are some programs that should be present on our system before installing Python. In fact, Python can be installed without these programs, but if you do not install these programs, you will not be able to take advantage of some of Python's features. These programs include:

tcl-dev

tk-dev

zlib1g-dev

ncurses-dev

libreadl-dev

libdb-dev

libgdbm-dev

libzip-dev

libssl-dev

libsqlite3-dev

libbz2-dev

liblz on-dev

You can install these programs through the package manager of the GNU / Linux distribution you are using.

Note that only package names and the number of packages required may vary between deployments. The above list applies to Ubuntu. For example, the package name given above as **tcl-dev** is simply referred to as tcl in another distribution, or some of the above packages is already installed in the distribution you are using, so you may need to install fewer dependencies.

In Ubuntu, you can install all the above packages with the following command:

sudo apt-get install tcl-dev tk-dev zlib1g-dev ncurses-dev libreadline-dev libdb-dev libgdbm-dev libzip-dev libssl-dev libsqlite3-dev libbz2-dev liblzma-dev

After installing the above programs, we go to

https://www.python.org/ftp/python/3.7.0. At this address, we click on the link labeled 'Python-3.7.0.tar.xz' to download the compressed installation file to our computer.

Then we unpack this compressed file. We go into the opened folder, and we give the first command there:

./configure

This command performs the necessary steps to install the Python programming language on your system. The basic task of this script is to check whether your system is suitable for the installation of the Python programming language, and whether the software required for compilation is installed on your system. This script also creates a file called Makefile, which describes how the construction process will be carried out in the next step.

Meanwhile, the ./ sign at the beginning of this command allows you to run a script called configure in the current directory. If you just configuregive the command, the operating system will look for this script in the PATH directories and will fail to find it.

./configure After completing the command without error, the second command is:

make

Here is actually ./configureoccurring with the command Makefile file named maker we have run through a program called. makeis a system command. When you run this command without parameters as above, the makecommand looks for a Makefile file in the current directory and executes it if it exists. If the ./configurecommand we executed in the previous step failed, the above command will not work because there will not be a Makefile file in the directory make. Therefore, we need to follow the output of the commands we gave during the compilation process and make sure that the command terminated properly before proceeding to the next stage.

makeThe task is to build and create files that will be copied to various parts of the system during the installation of the Python programming language on your system. This command may take a long time to complete, depending on the capacity of the computer you are using.

make After the command is completed, you may see a warning message to the last lines of the command output:

Python build finished, but the necessary bits to build these modules were not found:

[where missing names of modules or modules are listed]

Here, Python warns us that some packages are missing from our system. You may see one or more packages missing in the warning message. If so, we need to install all packages that are reported missing.

After installing the required package or packages, we makerun the command again, don't worry, the makesecond time we give the command, it won't take as long as the first one to complete. If the above warning message disappears when you run this command for the second time, you can proceed with the following command:

sudo make altinstall

GNU / Linux users who have previously compiled programs from the source may have gone to makeissue the command after the command. But note here that we use the command instead. command allows you to include the version number in folders and files when installing Python. This means that the newly installed Python does not delete and overwrite the old version of Python3 on the system, and two different versions may exist side by side. If you replace it, you can overwrite and delete files and directories from an old Python3 version that already exists on your system, making that version unusable. This can lead to unexpected problems in the system. You should never miss this important

detail.make installmake installmake altinstallmake altinstallmake altinstallmake install

If you have not received any error messages in any of the build steps, the installation has been successfully completed and the Python 3.x version of the programming language has been installed on your system.

Installation as an Unauthorized User

Of course, you need to have root rights to command and install Python. But if you don't have these rights on the system you're using, you can't install Python like this. You can only install Python in your home directory ( ) on a system where you have restricted rights .sudo make altinstall$HOME

If you are going to install Python as an unauthorized user, you should first check if the above mentioned Python dependencies are installed on your system. If any version of Python is already installed on the system you are using, these dependencies are probably already installed. If not, you will either ask the system administrator to install them, or you will install these dependencies one by one in your own home directory. If you cannot persuade the system administrator to install these dependencies, you can install them manually with the help of information available online. However this process will take a lot of time and you will encounter many other dependencies during the process. So It's suggested you do what you can and convince the system administrator to set up dependencies... Of course, if you can convince the system administrator to install these dependencies, you might think you can persuade them to install any version of Python you want! But here we go on assuming that you will install Python yourself.

Unauthorized installation of Python is very similar to installing with root rights. There are only a few differences between them. For example, when installing Python as an unauthorized user, ./configureyou should issue the command:

./configure --prefix = $ HOME / python

Python root when you install the rights Python / usr directory will be installed under. However, since you are an unauthorized user, you cannot install anything in the / usr directory. That's why we install Python in a directory that we have write privileges with the —prefix parameter we give to the configure script. For example, the above command will allow Python to be installed in a folder called python in your home directory, not in / usr. Of course you can specify a different directory name instead of python. The point is that —prefix The directory name you give to parameter is a directory that you are authorized to write.

After executing this command, we makeissue the command normally, we then install Python in our home directory with the command (or case). Here command Notice that we 'use the drain. Because, as we said, you cannot use the command because you are not an authorized user .make installmake altinstallmake installsudosudo

When you install Python in a folder under your home directory in this way, you will see that all Python-related files are in that folder. Examine this folder carefully and try to become familiar with what is where. If possible, examine a version of Python installed with root rights to compare where the files are copied in two different installation types.

So we learned how to install the Python programming language on our computer. But at this point, without warning: Python is closely linked to many system tools, especially in some GNU / Linux distributions. So Python can be the backbone of the distribution you use. Therefore, compiling Python from the source may present some risks. If you are compiling Python from the source as described above, you should be aware of the risks you are facing. Also, if you are not experienced in compiling programs from source on GNU / Linux, and if the above explanations are confusing, for example, 'Where do I write these commands?' You should definitely use the Python version that came with your distribution. Because Python versions follow head-to-head, you can try Ubuntu GNU / Linux. You can easily find the latest versions of Python in Ubuntu's repositories.

Let's just make another little warning. From what we say about installation from source, it doesn't mean that Python should never be installed on GNU / Linux from the source. The purpose of the above caveats is to remind that the user should only be more careful when compiling Python from the source. For instance, the author of these lines prefers to use Python3 from the source in his Ubuntu system and he has no problems.

Since we have made these important warnings, we can continue our journey with peace of mind.

We will see how to run the new Python we have installed. But first let's see how Windows users can install Python3.

Windows Users

Python is not installed on any version of Windows. That's why Windows users will download and install Python from their site.

To do this,

we first go to http://www.python.org/downloads.

When you go to this address, you will see a button that says 'Download Python 3.7.0'. As we said before, if a Python version number starts with '2', that version belongs to the 2.x series, and if it starts with '3', it belongs to the 3.x series. Therefore this button contains the Python3 version.

We click this button. Clicking this button will download the .exe extension file to your computer. You can start the installation program by double-clicking this file.

If you want to choose the architecture and version of the Python version you will download, you can find and download the appropriate version from

https://www.python.org/ftp/python/3.7.0.

When you double-click the installation file, you will see the following boxes at the bottom of the window:

Install launcher for all users (recommended)

Add Python 3.7 to PATH

The first box is already selected. You can leave it that way. The second box pythonwill allow us to add Python to the path so that we can start Python by simply issuing the command. So we mark the second box there.

At the top of the same window you will see the following options:

-> Install Now

-> Customize Installation

Click on 'Install Now' to start the installation.

If you want to change where Python should be installed on the computer and change some other installation features, you can click on the section labeled 'Customize Installation'. In this book It is assumed that you have installed by clicking 'Install Now'.

While browsing through Python's official site, you may see an installation file called 'web-based installer' among the installation files. This installation file contains a setup program smaller than 1MB, which downloads and installs the files required for Python to run during the installation. So if you are going to install from this file, you will need an uninterrupted internet connection.

If you get an error while trying to install Python on Windows, your operating system is probably outdated. For example, to install Python on Windows 7, SP1 (Service Pack 1) must be installed. After installing Windows updates, try installing Python again.

Python Installation and Working Directory

As well as knowing how to install the Python programming language on the operating system we use, it is as important to know in which directory we install Python. Because some of the problems we will encounter during our programming adventure will require us to go to the directory where Python is installed, and in some programs we have written, we will need to perform various operations in the directory where Python is installed. In some cases, we may also need to determine where the current version of Python is running.

For these reasons, we need to know which directory Python is installed on.

The directory in which Python is installed on your operating system differs depending on how you install Python.

In GNU / Linux distributions, Python is usually installed in / usr / lib / python 3.7. But of course, if you have compiled Python from the source, you may have set the Python installation directory yourself by using the —prefix parameter you gave to the configure script during compilation.

If you have installed the Python programming language in Windows exactly as shown in this book, it will be installed in   the   Python

%LOCALAPPDATA%\Programs\Pythondirectory. However, if you have customized the installation by clicking the 'Customize Installation' button in the installation window and checked 'Install for all users', Python will be installed in the directory pointed to by the environment variables %PROGRAMFILES% or % PROGRAMFILES (x86) .

PART II

Interactive Python

Thanks to what we have learned so far, we know how to install and run the Python programming language on different systems. So when we run Python as described in the previous section, we realize that we will see a screen like this:

yazbel @ ubuntu: ~ $ # python3 [GCC 4.4.7 20120313 (Red Hat 4.4.7-3)] on linux Type "help", "copyright "," Credits "or" license "for more information. >>>

So far, we have chosen to call this screen a Python command line. You can continue to use this name from now on. But technically, this screen interactive shell (interactive shellIt is useful to know that the name. The interactive shell is a top layer in which we can relate to, or interact with, the Python programming language. The interactive shell allows us to test the code that we will use in our original program. This is kind of like a test ground. For example, if you want to try to see if a Python code works, or how it works, what results, this screen is a very useful tool. This environment is also an invaluable tool, especially for beginners to become familiar with this programming language. In this section, we will do some work on the interactive shell and get familiar with Python.

In the meantime, as we said in the previous section, we keep in mind that this environment is different from what we call the system command line. Then, as we said, system commands are given at the system command line, and Python commands are given at the Python command line (ie in the interactive shell). For example, and it is a system command, if you attempt to issue these commands in the interactive shell, Python will display an error message because they are not Python commands. For example, if you command it in Python's interactive shell, you get an error like this:echo %PATH%cd Desktopdirlscd Desktop

```
>>> cd  Desktop
```

```
  File "<stdin>" , line 1
    cd Desktop
            ^
SyntaxError : invalid syntax
```

Because it is not a Python command. So we can't give this command in Python's interactive shell. We can only issue this command on the command line of the operating system we use.cd Desktop

What were we saying? The interactive shell is a very convenient tool to try / test one or several lines of code. If you want, let's not talk about it anymore. Because as you use the interactive shell, you will understand what a blessing it is. My companions, especially those who have worked with compiled programming languages, will not have tears when they see the power of the interactive shell.

Different operating systems py3, , or we explained that we can command the Python command-line access, giving in detail in previous lessons. If you're having trouble accessing the interactive shell, It's suggested you revisit old issues.py -3python3python

Before you start working on the interactive shell, let us clarify one important issue: we have successfully run the interactive shell. What if we want to get out of this shell? Of course you can leave this environment by pressing the cross key directly on the window. But there must be a way to do this without resorting to brute force, right?

There are several different ways to exit the interactive shell:

Pressing the cross button on the window (brute force)

Press Ctrl + Z , then press Enter (Windows)

Pressing Ctrl + Z (GNU / Linux)

Before the F6 key, then Enter to press (Windows)

quit()type and press Enter (All operating systems)

import sys; sys.exit() command (All operating systems)

Among these different methods, you can choose whichever comes easy for you. The author of these lines is numbered 2 in Windows; In GNU / Linux, he prefers option 3.

First Steps in Interactive Shell

Now that we have learned how to run and leave the interactive shell in Python, we can now take the first steps in the Python programming language through the interactive shell.

Now let's run the interactive shell again in accordance with our system. When we run the interactive shell, the >>> sign on the screen indicates that Python is ready to receive commands from us. Immediately after this >>> , we will write our Python code with no spaces .

The 'no space' part here is important. One of the most common mistakes for newbies to Python is that they leave a space between the >>> sign and the command. If you leave a space like this, the code you write will give an error.

Let's do a simple experiment. Immediately after the >>> sign, let's write the following command with no spaces:

>>> "Hello Cruel World!"

In the meantime, you will not enter the >>> sign that appears in the above codes . We have placed this sign to represent the appearance of the interactive shell. After you type the line "Hello Cruel World!" You will press the Enter button directly.

When we type this command and press Enter, we should have got the following output:

'Hello Cruel World!'

So we have written our first Python program, albeit sketchy...

Probably this code hasn't aroused the slightest excitement in you. Even writing such code may be pointless to you. But even that tiny piece of code gives us very important clues about the Python programming language. Let's take a look at this one-line code...

Introduction to Strings

As said, the tiny piece of code we've written above may not excite you, but it actually contains important information about the Python programming language and its structure.

Technically speaking, the phrase "Hello Cruel World! Yukarıda we wrote above is a series of characters. This is called a string in English and is a very important concept for programming. As you can easily understand from the name of the concept, we call elements consisting of one or more characters as strings.

Character sequences will emerge throughout our entire programming adventure. So the sooner we learn this concept, the better.

But what is the benefit of having a string of data? So what happened to us that the above sentence has not been in the string?

In Python, it is extremely important to know what type of data you currently have because the type that a data belongs to determines what you can and can't do with that data. In Python, each data type has certain properties. Therefore, if we do not know the type of data we have, we cannot use that data effectively in our programs. Here is an example of the character series "Hello Cruel World! Yukarıda which we have given above. Python has other data types other than strings. We will look at other data types in a little while.

Notice that we have shown the character string "Hello Cruel World! Içinde in quotes. This is very important information. If we do not put this sentence in quotes, our program will give an error:

```
>>> Hello Cruel World!
```

```
  File "<stdin>", line 1
    Hello Cruel World!
          ^
SyntaxError: invalid syntax
```

Quotation marks are already distinctive to strings. In Python, everything you show in quotes is a string. For example, this is a string:

```
>>> "a"
```

As you can see, a single-character element shown in quotes is also included in the string class in Python.

For example, this is a hollow string:

```
>>> ""
```

Here's a string containing a space character...

```
>>> ""
```

We pay attention to the difference between the two: In Python, 'empty string' and 'one string of strings' are two different concepts. As its name implies, empty strings are strings that contain no characters (in other words, 'elements'). Strings of one (or more) spaces are strings that contain spaces. So one of these strings is empty and the other is full. But in the end, both are strings. You may feel like we're wasting time on a rather meaningless topic right now, but it's sure this is one of the major stumbling points for beginners in Python programming.

Let us give you a few examples to get used to the character strings:

```
>>> "Apple"

'Apple'

>>> "Guido Van Rossum"

'Guido Van Rossum'

>>> "Python programming language"

'Python programming language'

>>> "life time"

'Ömnhbgfgh'

>>> "$ 5 &"
```

'& $ 5'

>>> ""

"

>>> ""

"

The above examples are all strings. Note that all of the above strings have a common property in quotation marks. As we said, quotation marks are a distinctive feature of strings.

So how can you be sure that a data is a string?

If you have any doubts about whether or not any data is a string, you type()can use a function called to query the type of data. We use this function:

```
>>> type ( "Apple" )
```

```
<class 'str'>
```

Don't let this 'function' confuse you. Since we will examine the functions in detail in the future, type()it is enough for you to know that the expression is a function for now. Moreover, when it is time to describe the function in detail, you will have already learned a lot about functions.

Our goal here is to check the type of item called ma Apple " . type()Note that we specify the item to be checked between the parentheses of the function. (Values specified in parentheses of functions are called parameters in technical language.)

The part that concerns us in the above output is the expression 'str' at the end. As you can imagine, this is an abbreviation for string. We said that this word means character sequence in Turkish. So, by looking at the above output, we can say that "Apple" is a string.

type() it's recommended you to digest the subject thoroughly by making some experiments yourself. For example, you can start by checking which class "½ {656 $ # gfd girdi is in.

What can we do with strings? We can't do much with strings because our knowledge of Python is limited at the moment, but as our knowledge increases in the future, we will be tight with strings.

In fact, even though our knowledge is limited, we are still in a situation where we cannot do a few things with character sequences. For example, we can combine strings with our current knowledge and some simple pieces that will become familiar to you as soon as you see them:

```
>>> "yazbel" + ".com"
```

```
'Yazbel.co'
```

Notice how we can combine strings here using the + sign. When we combine the two strings with the + sign, I would like to draw your attention to the fact that there are no spaces between the strings. We can see this more clearly in the following example:

```
>>> "Euphrates" + "Specific"
```

```
'Fıratözgül'
```

As you can see, these two strings were interconnected without spaces. You can use several different methods to add spaces:

```
>>> "Euphrates" + "" + "Specific"
```

'Fırat Özgül'

Here we placed a space character between two strings. You can achieve the same effect:

```
>>> "Euphrates" + "Specific"
```

Here, too, we placed a space at the beginning of the specific character string and achieved the desired output.

By the way, you don't necessarily have to use the + sign to concatenate strings . You + do not use the sign is also smart enough to understand what you want your character to combine the Python series:

```
>>> "www" "." "google" "." "com"
```

'Www.google.co'

But as you can see, using the + sign makes your code more legible.

In addition to the + sign, we can use the * (cross) sign along with the strings. Then we get the effect:

>>> "w" * 3

'Www'

>>> "slow" * 2

'slowly '

>>> "-" * 10

'----------'

```
>>> "remote" + "" * 5 + "too far ..."
```

'far too far ...'

As you can see, we are able to combine very simple pieces to produce complex outputs. For example, in the last example, we added the 5 space characters ( ) to the "remote karakter character string and then the " too far ... diz character string." " * 5

Here we see two new tools called + and *. These are actually arithmetic operators used with numbers. Normally, the + operator is used for aggregation and the * operator is used for multiplication. But in the above examples, the 'sign' of the + sign; because the * sign means 'repetition', we can sometimes use these two operators with strings. There are also - (minus) and / (over) operators. However, we cannot use these signs with strings.

We will examine the strings in full detail in a later section. So let's take a break for now.

Introduction to Numbers

It's been said that Python has a number of data types, and strings are just one of those data types. Apart from the string as a data type, we mentioned a little while ago on the occasion of arithmetic operators, an 'issue' (number) has a data type called.

There is no need to describe what numbers mean. These are the numbers we know. E.g:

>>> 23

23

>>> 4567

4567

>>> 2.3

2.3

>>> (10 + 2 j)

(10 + 2j)

Python has different subtypes of numbers. For example, integers, floating-point numbers, complex numbers...

In the above examples 23 and 4567 being an integer. In English, such numbers are called integers.

2.3 is a floating point number or float. Note, however, that we use a period, not a comma, as a point separator in floating-point numbers.

In the end we saw 10 + 2 j The number is a complex number (complex). However, if you are not intensely involved in mathematics, complex numbers do not appear.

Now that we know the numbers, we can use the interactive shell as a simple calculator:

```
>>> 5 + 2
```

7

```
>>> 25 * 25
```

625

```
>>> 5 / 2
```

2.5

```
>>> 10 - 3
```

7

In the examples above, we have just mentioned the arithmetic operators. So don't think you're alienating them. But let us list these operators and their tasks:

operators   Task

+   collection

-   extraction

*   impact

/   chamber

One thing you should notice is the following examples: We used quotes to define strings. However, there are ro quotation marks on the numbers. As we said before, quotation marks are a distinguishing feature of strings. Everything you show in quotes in Python is a string. Let's look at the following examples:

>>> 34657

34657

This is a number. What about that?

```
>>> "34657"
```

```
'34657'
```

This is a string. Let's type()query the type of this data with the help of the function we have just learned :

```
>>> type ( 34657 )
```

```
<class 'int'>
```

Where 'int' English phrase " integer " are an abbreviation for the word integer. So 34657 is an integer. Let's look at this:

```
>>> type ( "34657" )
```

```
<class 'str'>
```

As you can see, when we put the number 34657 in quotation marks, it no longer becomes a number and becomes a string. At the moment, this may seem like an insignificant detail, but it is actually an extremely important issue. You can see the effects of this in the following examples:

```
>>> 23 + 65
```

88

Here we have normally added two numbers together.

Look at this:

```
>>> "23" + "65"
```

'2365'

Here, Python only writes two strings side by side; So he combined them. In Python, "23" and 23 are different. "23" is a string, while 23 is a number. The same applies to "65" and 65 . So for Python, there is no difference between "65" and "Hello Cruel World!" Both of these fall into the string class. However, 65 and "65 dır are different. While 65 is a number, "65" is a string.

This information is especially important in arithmetic operations. Let us show you on the following examples:

>>> 45 + "45"

Traceback (most recent call last):

File "<stdin>" , line 1 , in <module>

TypeError : unsupported operand type (s) for +: 'int' and 'str'

As you can see, the above codes give an error. This is because we try to add a number (45) to a string ("45"). Never forget that arithmetic operations are only performed between numbers. Arithmetic operations cannot be performed with strings.

Let's look at this:

```
>>> 45 + 45
```

```
90
```

These codes work properly. Because here we have arithmetic two numbers and we succeeded.

Finally, the following example:

```
>>> "45" + "45"
```

```
'4545'
```

Note that the + operator does not mean aggregation here. This operator assumes the task of joining two strings. So the above example is no different from the following example:

```
>>> "yazbel." + "com"
```

```
Yazbel.co'
```

What we do in these two examples is to combine strings.

As you can see, if the values to the left and right of the + operator are strings, these operators combine these two values. But if these values are numbers, the + operator adds these values to each other arithmetically.

The * operator does something similar to the + operator. That is, if the * operator encounters a number and a string, it repeats that string by the given number. For example:

>>> "w" * 3

'Www'

Here, the operator * repeats a string (ilgili w ") and a number (3), repeating the string by the corresponding number. So "w" repeats the string 3 times.

Let's look at this:

```
>>> 25 * 3
```

75

In this case, the * operator performs the operation between two numbers and multiplies these values with each other arithmetically and enables us to obtain the value 75.

As you can see, knowing the type of data we have at that moment is really important. Because if we do not know the type of data we have, we cannot predict how we can achieve results.

Thus, we learned the difference between strings and numbers. This information may seem trivial to you, but actually understanding the difference between strings and numbers means that you have learned a significant part of the Python programming language. Even in the most complex programs you'll write in the future, you'll find that sometimes the reason your program doesn't work (or worse, it's wrong) is that you mix strings and numbers. So I recommend that you do not defeat (and impatience cr haste) any of the information you have learned here.

Variables

Now imagine: You are writing a program that asks for a user name and password for registration. In this program, the total length of the user name and password that can be specified will not exceed 40 characters.

When writing this program, the first step you need to do is to check the length of the user-specified user name and password individually.

For example, the user has set a username like:

firat_ozgul_1980

Let the user set the password:

RT # $% 65 hgfuy56123

First of all, we need to know the length of these data from the user one by one, so that we can check whether the data exceeds the limit of 40 characters.

So how do we measure the length of this data? Of course, we will not count the letters in the data manually. Instead, we will use a tool provided by the Python programming language. What is this vehicle?

Remember, a few pages ago type()we mentioned a function called. The task of this function was to tell us what type of data it was. Just type()like in Python len()there is another function called. The function of this function is to measure the length of strings (and other data types as we will see later). So using this function we can find out how many characters a string consists of.

We don't yet know how to get data from the user. But for now we can say: When we get any data from the user in Python, that data will come to us as a string. So, assuming that we've received the above username and password from the user, this data comes to us as follows:

"Firat_ozgul_1980"

and:

"RT 65 # $% hgfuy56123"

As you can see, the data we get is in quotation marks. So these are strings. Now let's len()measure the length of these strings using the function mentioned above .

Like as said, len()it's just type()like a function. Therefore, len()the use of the type()function is very similar to the use of the function. Just as the type()function tells us the type of parameters we give it, the len()function tells us the length of the parameters we give it .

Look carefully:

>>> len ("firat_ozgul_1980")

16

>>> len ("rT% 65 # $ hGfUY56123")

17

So, in the character series "firat_ozgul_1980 16 , 16 ; The character string isinde rT% 65 # $ hGfUY56123 var had 17 characters. What we want is that the total length of these two values does not exceed 40 characters. To check this, all we have to do is add the length of these two values together. So:

```
>>> len ( "firat_ozgul_1980" )  +  len ( "rT% 65 # $
hGfUY56123" )
```

The result will be 33. This means that the user has not exceeded the 40- character limit. Then our program can accept this username and password...

By the way, maybe you did, maybe you didn't, but here we are facing a very important situation. As you can see the len()function is sending us a valuable data of numbers. Let's confirm it if you like:


```
>>> type ( len ( "firat_ozgul_1980" ))
```


```
<class 'int'>
```

len() Since the function sends us a number of data, we can add the values we obtain from this function:


```
>>> len ( "firat_ozgul_1980" )  +  len ( "rT% 65 # $
hGfUY56123")
```


```
33
```

If the len()function gave us a string rather than a number, for example, we would not be able to arithmetically add the values obtained from this function directly to each other as above. In this case, when we try to collect these two data, the + operator 16 and 17 would give us a result like '1617' by combining these values with each other instead of values together.

As said, it is very important to understand the concept of data type in Python and to know what type of data we have at the moment. Otherwise, it is inevitable that we make mistakes in our programs.

If you find the above-mentioned things confusing, don't worry. After a few episodesinput() we talk about a function named a you will understand things much more clearly.

Soon len()We'll continue to talk about its function in a while, but if you want, let's talk about a very important issue.

We just gave you an example:

```
>>> len ( "firat_ozgul_1980" )
```

16

>>> len ("rT% 65 # $ hGfUᵛ56123")

17

>>> len ("firat_ozgul_1980") + len ("rT% 65 # $ hGfUY56123")

These codes do exactly what we want. But do you think that the above code is very disturbing?

Note that we have repeatedly written the data we use in the examples above, whenever we need it in the program. Thus, within the same program twice "firat_ozgul_1980" ; we had to write "rT 65% # $ hGfUY56123 iki twice . But wouldn't it be much better to assign this data to a variable instead of writing it over and over again whenever we need it in our programs and use that variable when necessary? Probably...

What is this variable?

In Python, the names given to values in a program are called variables. Let's give an example:

>>> n = 5

Here we assign the number 5 to a variable. Our variable is n. Also note that we use the = sign to assign the number 5 to a variable. We conclude that the = sign is used for value assignment in the Python programming language.

n = 5By assigning the value 5 to a variable named n with the help of a command like this, it is enough to call this variable n whenever we need 5 :

>>> n

5

>>> n * 10

50

>>> n / 2

2.5

As you can see, 5 After assigning a value to a variable, these five places we need only use the value of the variable, the variable's name we use Python can be automatically put into place. So after defining a variable named n with the command, it is enough to call variable n whenever we need 5. Python o 5n = 5 automatically replaces value.

Now let's define another variable called pi:

>>> pi = 3.14

Add the value of this variable pi and the value of variable n:

>>> pi + n

8:14

As you can see, instead of rewriting the values each time, it is much more practical to assign them to a variable and use it where necessary.

We can do the same for our program:

>>> username = "firat_ozgul_1980"

>>> password = "rt 65% # $ hgfuy56123"

Since we now assign a name to the corresponding values using the = sign, that is, assigning these values to variables, we can use the variable names that we specify instead of typing the values themselves where we need to use those values. E.g:

>>> man (username)

16

```
>>> len ( password )
```

17

```
>>> man ( username ) + man ( password )
```

33

```
>>> k_adı_uzunlug of = man ( username )
>>> type ( k_adı_uzunlug a )
```

<class 'int'>

As you can see, the use of variables makes our work much easier.

Variable Name Determination Rules

In the Python programming language, the number of words that we can specify as a variable name is almost unlimited. So we can use almost every word as the variable name. But there are still some rules to consider when setting the variable name. Some of these rules are mandatory and some are only recommendations.

Now let's examine these rules one by one:

1. Variable names cannot begin with a number. So the following usage is wrong:

>>> 3 _kilo_elma = "5 TL"

2. Variable names cannot begin with arithmetic operators. So the following usage is wrong:

>>> + value = 4568

3. Variable names must begin with either an alphabet letter or an _ sign:

>>> _value = 4568

```
>>> value = 4568
```

4. You can use Turkish characters within variable names. However, you may want to avoid using Turkish characters in variable names in case of unexpected compatibility problems in the future.

5. You cannot use the following words as the variable name:

['False' , 'None' , 'True' , 'and' , 'as' , ' assert ' , ' async ' , ' await ' , ' break ' , ' class' , 'continue' , 'def' , ' del ' ,

' elif ' , ' else ' , ' except ' , ' finally ' , ' fr ' , ' from ' , , ' not ' , ' o ' , 'pass' , 'raise' , 'return' ' global ' , ' if ' , ' import ', 'in' , 'is' , 'lambda' , 'nonlocal'

, 'try' , 'while' , 'with' , 'yield']

These are words that have special meaning in Python. The interactive shell does not already allow you to use these words as variable names. For example:

```
>>> elif  =  "pretty girl"


  File "<stdin>" , line 1

    elif  =  "nice girl"

      ^

SyntaxError : invalid syntax


>>> as  =  "square"


  File "<stdin>" , line 1

    as  =  "square"

      ^

SyntaxError : invalid syntax


>>> False  =  45


  File "<stdin>" , line 1

SyntaxError : assignment to keyword
```

But as we will see, if you try to use these words as the variable name when writing your programs to a file, your program will produce very difficult errors to detect.

In the meantime, of course you are not expected to memorize the above list in a snap. As you learn the Python programming language, you will be able to recognize specific words at a glance. You can also access the above list at any time by giving the following commands if you wish:

>>> import keyword

>>> keyword . kwlist

['False', 'None', 'True', 'and', 'as',' assert ',' async ',' await ','
break ',' class', 'continue', 'def', ' del ',

' elif ',' else ',' except ',' finally ',' for ',' from ',' global ',' if ','
import ',' in ',' is', 'lambda' , 'nonlocal',

'not', 'or', 'pass', 'raise', 'return', 'try', 'while', 'with', 'yield']

A question to you: How many words are in this list?

In the face of this question, I pass on my gratitude to my friends who attempt to count the words in the list one by one... You must know very well which tool we can use for this kind of work:

```
>>> len ( keyword . kwlist )
```

35

You also know that we can write these codes:

```
>>> banned_words = keyword . kwlist
>>> len ( forbidden_words) )
```

35

In the meantime, you may not yet understand some of the above code. Don't worry at all. The reason we give the above code is to show you how to reach words that cannot be used as variable names. After one or two chapters, you will be able to understand the codes we write here.

As we understand from the output of the codes given above, the total 35 have to avoid using a variable name words in...

6. In addition to the above words, you should not use the names of functions and similar tools of the Python programming language as variable names. For example, in programs you write, do not name your variables type or len. Because 'type' and 'len' are the two important functions of Python. For example , if you name a variable type , you type()can no longer use the function in that program:

>>> type = 3456

In this example, we have defined a variable named type . Now, for example, let's try to use the function to check the type of the word "appletype() ::

>>> type ("apple")

Traceback (most recent call last):

  File "<stdin>" , line 1 , in <module>

TypeError : 'int' object is not callable

As you can see, the type()function no longer works. Because you type()made the function unusable using the word 'type' as a variable name .

To get rid of this, you can turn the interactive shell off and on again. Or, if you don't want to turn off the interactive shell, you can choose to disable the type variable with the following command :

>>> del type

So, you deleted the type variable with the command (as you might expect, the abbreviation of delete) . The word 'type' will now call the function:deltype()

>>> type ("apple")

7. When specifying variable names, no spaces can be left between the words that make up the variable. So the following usage is wrong:

>>> user name = "yazbel"

We can define the above variable as follows:

>>> username = "yazbel"

Or something like:

>>> username = "yazbel"

8. When determining variable names, paying attention to the variable name to describe the value of the variable as much as possible will increase the legibility of our codes. For example:

>>> number of staff = 45

The above is the name of a variable that corresponds to the value it defines. The following is a proper variable name, but not descriptive enough:

>>> number = 45

9. Variable names must be neither too short nor too long. For example, the variable name does not give the reader the idea of the meaning of the variable value:

>>> a = 345542353

The following variable name is unnecessarily long:

>>> türkiye_büyük_millet_meclisi_milletvekili_sayı of   =
600

It is essential to keep the length of variable names at a reasonable level:

>>> tbmm_mv_number = 600

All of the above examples show us that variables in Python consist of names assigned to values. Variables provide great convenience to the programs we write. For example 123432456322 is a number or as a "Republic of Turkey Ministry of Labor and Social Security" should a string of characters such as instead of typing anywhere individually by hand, by assigning them to a variable, it can only use this variable name is a much more sensible business.

In addition, when you already receive data from the user in the future, you will have to assign it to a variable in order to use it in the program you are writing. That is why it is very useful to understand and understand the concept of variable in Python.

Application Examples

Let's do a few small exercises to consolidate the information we have provided above, while introducing you to some very important new information about the Python programming language.

Let's say we want to write a program that calculates our monthly travel costs. Suppose we have the following data:

We do not work on Saturdays and Sundays.

So we work 22 days a month.

The cost of the vehicle we use to go from home to work is 1.5 TL

The fee we use to return home from work 1.4 TL

In order to calculate our monthly travel costs, it is enough to collect the round trip and return costs and multiply them by the number of days we work. Based on this information, we can generate a formula to calculate our monthly travel costs:

expense = number of days x (departure fee + return fee)

Let's make it a Python program:

```
>>> 22 * ( 1.5 + 1.4 )
```

63.8

That means we have a road trip of 63.8 TL in a month.

By the way, something in the example above must have caught your attention. When performing the arithmetic operation, we have enclosed some numbers in parentheses. The mathematical rules that we are used to do arithmetic operations in Python are valid. That is, for example, if simultaneous division, subtraction, addition and multiplication operations are to be performed, the order of priority will be first division and multiplication, then addition and subtraction. Of course you can change the order of this operation with the help of brackets.

According to this, if we do not use parentheses in the program that calculates the cost of the road above, according to the procedure priority rules, Python will multiply 22 by 1.5 first and add the result to 1.4, so the result will be wrong. In order to get the right result here, we have to add 1.5 to 1.4 and multiply the result by 22. We get this ranking with the help of brackets.

Again, in the example program above, we actually followed a very inefficient path. As you can see, in this program we enter all the values one by one by hand. For example, if we want to use the value of 22 corresponding to the number of days worked elsewhere, we have to manually enter the same number again. For example, let's calculate how many days we work:

```
>>> 22 * 12
```

264

As you can see, we needed the number 22 here. In fact, entering the values manually each time over and over again is an undesirable method because it increases the risk of mistakes and gives us extra work. Instead, it would make more sense to give the name 22 a name and use it where necessary. So just like the user and password example, it's much wiser to assign the data to a variable first:

```
>>> day = 22
>>> departure cost = 1.5
>>> return cost = 1.4
>>> day * ( departure cost + return cost )
```

63.8

Since we assign all values to variables, we can now use these variables anywhere. For example, if we want to find out how many days we work in a year, we can use the day variable described above instead of manually typing the value:

```
>>> day * 12
```

264

If the number of working days per month changes in the future, we only need to change the value of the day variable:

>>> days = 23

>>> days * (departure + return + fee)

66.7

>>> day * 12

276

If we had to manually type the values wherever necessary instead of assigning variables in this way, if we had to make any changes to these values, we would have to find all the relevant values in the program and change them one by one:

>>> 23 * (1.6 + 1.5)

71.3

```
>>> 23 * 12
```

276

The concept of variable may not seem to make sense to you at this time. But when we save our programs to the file in the future, these variables will appear as much more useful tools.

Let us make another example and make sure that the above information is well placed in our heads. For example, let's write a program that calculates (approximately) the area of a circle.

First diameter by defining a variable called Let's set the diameter of the circle:

```
>>> Diameter = 16
```

Using this value, we can calculate the radius of our circle. Diameter for this we only need to take half the value of variable:

```
>>> Radius = diameter / 2
```

The number of pi 3.14159Let's take the .

```
>>> pi = 3.14159
```

The area formula of a circle is (pi) r 2 :

```
>>> Area = Pi * ( Radius * Radius )
```

Finally, we can print the value of the field variable:

```
>>> area
```

201.06176

So we calculated the approximate area of a circle. Let's see our program as a tidy:

```
>>> diameter = 16

>>> radius = diameter / 2

>>> pi = 3.14159

>>> area = pi * ( radius * radius )

>>> area
```

201.06176

You see, the variables make our job easier. If we did not use a variable in the above program, our code would look like this:

```
>>> 3.14159 * (( 16th / 2 ) * ( 16th / 2 ))
```

201.06176

These codes are for single use only. If, for example, you need to change the diameter of the circle in the example above, you need to manually change the two places. But when you use variables, you only need to change the value of the diameter variable. Also, when you do not use a variable, you must keep that value in mind throughout the program. For example, the diameter instead of using the variables needed everywhere 16 If you use the value of these 16 have to constantly keep the value of your mind. But if you assign this value to a variable in the first place, it's easier to keep in mind where you need to use the value of 16 . diameter name remember .

In the meantime, let us introduce you to a new operator. So far in Python, addition (+), subtraction (-), multiplication (*), division (/) and value assignment (=) operators in . But the last example above requires us to learn another operator ...

Let's look at this example again:

area = pi * (radius * radius)

Radius here we multiplied this value by itself to square the variable. In fact, it is a very reasonable and reasonable method. Multiply the value by itself to find the square. If we wanted to find the cube of a number, we would multiply it three times:

```
>>> 3 * 3 * 3
```

27

What if we want to calculate the fifth force of a number? We're going to multiply that number five times? Isn't that just a mediocre way?

Of course, to calculate any force of a number, we will not multiply that number by its force. Python has a separate operator (and function) for such 'force calculations'.

First, let's talk about the operator that allows us to calculate the force.

in Python has an operator named ** . The task of this operator is to calculate the strength of a number. For example, a number of 2nd forces, or in other words, if we want to calculate the square you can write code like this:

```
>>> 12 ** 2
```

144

Here number 2 of 12. calculated the power of the , that is the square. Let's apply this information to the above formula:

```
>>> area = pi * ( radius ** 2 )
```

Of course we can use this operator to calculate any force of any number. For example 23 calculate the cube of the number (that is, force 3):

```
>>> 23 ** 3
```

12167

You can also use the same operator to calculate the square root of a number. As a result of a number 0.5 -th power, that is the square root of the number of:

```
>>> 144 ** 0.5
```

12.0

As you can see, this operator is a very useful tool for force calculation operations. But if we want, we can also use a special function for the same job. Name of this functionpow() .

So how do we use this function?

What we learned before type()and len()how we use the functionspow() function in the same way as we have we use it.

type()and len()remember that we used the functions together with a number of parameters. The pow()function also takes a number of parameters.

We used the functions we learned before with a single parameter. pow()function takes a total of three different parameters. But usually this function is only used with two parameters.

We use this function:

>>> pow (12 , 2)

144

>>> pow (23 , 3)

12167

>>> pow (144 , 0.5)

12.0

As you see, pow() the first parameter of the function shows the actual number, and the second parameter shows the strength of this number.

In the meantime, keep in mind that we separate the parameters that we specify in parentheses with commas.

As said, the pow()function takes a third parameter that is not used much. The third parameter of this function is used as follows. Look carefully:

>>> pow (16 , 2 , 2)

0

This command means:

16 volumes of the 2 nd force and the calculated number 2 'to divide, show the remaining number of division!

The 2nd force of the number 16 is 256. When we divide the number 256 by 2, the remainder of the division is 0. So the number 256 is exactly divided by 2...

Here's another example:

```
>>> pow ( 11 , 3 , 4 )
```

3

It means that 11 of the number 3 which forces 1331 Number 4 'is to divide the number of remaining Divides three have i ...

As we said, the pow()function is usually used with only two parameters. The use of the third parameter is very narrow.

Some Tips on Variables

Now that we know what the variable means, we can give you some hints about the variables.

Defining Variables with Same Value

Now let me ask you a question: How can we define two variables of the same value? So for example the value 4, how do we determine two different variables whose?

You may have come up with a solution:

```
>>> a = 4
```

```
>>> b = 4
```

So they both have a value of 4 we have defined two different variables named and b, both of which. This is a completely valid method. However, there is an easier way to do this in Python. Let's see:

```
>>> a = b = 4
```

These codes function exactly the same as the previous one. So both codes have a value of 4 define variables and b:

```
>>> a
```

4

```
>>> b
```

4

Using this information, you can, for example, assign the number of days each month in a year to the month names:

>>> January = March = May = July = August = October = December = 31

>>> April = June = September = November = 30

>>> February = 28

Thus, a snap value of 31 with seven variables, the value cf 30 with four variables, the value of 28, we have identified one variable. You know how to get the value of these variables:

>>> cooker

31

>>> June

30

```
>>> February
```

```
28
```

```
>>> May
```

```
31
```

```
>>> October
```

```
31
```

```
>>> September
```

```
30
```

If Python did not have the ability to assign a single value to more than one variable at a time, we would have written the above code:

>>> January = 31

>>> February = 28

>>> March = 31

>>> April = 30

>>> May = 31

>>> June = 30

>>> July = 31

>>> August = 31

>> > September = 30

>>> October = 31

>>> November = 30

>>> December = 31

How you use these variables in a program is entirely up to your imagination. For example, we can write a program that calculates the natural gas bill by using these variables.

We immediately take over the last natural gas bill (eg March) and we obtain the following data from this bill:

According to the March natural gas bill, the measured volume is 346 m 3 . That means a total of 346 m 3 in a month spent natural gas in .

The invoice amount was 273.87 TL. So the cost of consuming 346 m 3 of natural gas is 273.87 TL. Let's define our variables accordingly:

>>> monthly_price = 346

>>> invoice amount = 273.87

Using this information, we can calculate the unit price of natural gas. Our formula should be:

>>> unit_price = invoice_account / monthly_price

>>> unit_price

0.7915317919075144

Thus, the m 3 price of natural gas (with taxes) corresponds to 0.79 TL.

At this point, we need to calculate our average daily natural gas consumption:

```
>>> daily_supply = monthly_supply / march
>>> daily_supply
```

11.161290322580646

This means that the average daily average in March is 11 m 3 consumed natural gas.

Using all this information, we can estimate the next bill in April:

```
>>> april_fatur = unit_price * daily_safety * april
>>> april_fatur
```

265.03548387096777

February invoice can be:

```
>>> february = unit_price * daily_safety * february

>>> february
```

247.36645161290326

Here you can perform further operations by changing the value of different variables. For example, the value of daily_profile is 15 for practical purposes. , you can update your calculations accordingly by.

As you can see, being able to define more than one variable at the same time makes our work much easier.

Let's give you another hint about variables...

Swap the Value of Variables

Let's say you have a database where you keep the titles of the personnel in your workplace. In this database, relationships similar to this are defined:

```
>>> osman = "Research and Development Manager"

>>> mehmet = "Project Officer"
```

In the future, your employer may ask you to change the titles of Osman and Mehmet. In other words, Osman can be asked to make you Project Manager and Mehmet is Research and Development Manager.

You can easily fulfill this request of your boss in Python. Look carefully:

```
>>> osman , mehmet = mehmet , osman
```

Thus, in one move, you exchanged the titles of these two people. Let's look at the last state of the variables:

```
>>> osman
```

'Project manager

```
>>> mehmet
```

'Research and Development Manager'

As you can see, the value of osman variable to mehmet ; the value of the variable variable osman can successfully give the .

The above method is an important advantage of Python over other languages. To do this in other programming languages, you must define a temporary variable. So for example:

>>> osman = "Research and Development Manager"

>>> mehmet = "Project Officer"

These are the values we have. We now value Osman's value to Mehmet; We will transfer the value of Mehmet to Osman. To do this, we must first define a temporary variable:

>>> temporary = "Project Officer"

In this way, "Project Responsible" we have backed up the value of... With this process, we will not lose this value during the swap.

Now let's convey Osman's value to Mehmet:

```
>>> mehmet = osman
```

Now we have two Research and Development Managers:

```
>>> mehmet
```

'Research and Development Manager'

```
>>> osman
```

'Research and Development Manager'

As you can see, the value of değişken Project Officer " disappeared because we changed the value of mehmet variable to osman variable by using its code . But we did not lose this value because we previously assigned this value to the variable named temporary . Now to Osman temporarymehmet = osman , we can give value of the "Project Officer uğ that we keep in the variable:

```
>>> osman = temporary
```

Thus, we have realized the swap process we want. Let's check the latest situation:

```
>>> osman
```

'Project manager

```
>>> mehmet
```

'Research and Development Manager'

What a waste of time for a simple operation, isn't it? But as said, we don't have to deal with assigning such a temporary variable in Python. We can only trade the value of variables using the following formula:

```
a , b = b , a
```

In this way, the value of variable a to variable b; we give the value of variable b to a value. If we want to undo this process, we can use the same method as you can imagine:

b , a = a , b

Thus, we examined the subject of variables in detail. Also during this time len()andpow() has two new functions with ** have learned well from an operator.

Speaking of which, len()let's talk about some limitations of its function. As we said, we can use this function to calculate the total number of characters in strings. For example:

>>> word = "success"

>>> len (word)

12

However, we len()cannot use this function to measure the length of numbers:

>>> len (123456)

Traceback (most recent call last):

File "<stdin>" , line 1 , in <module>

TypeError : object of type 'int' has no len ()

As you see, len() function can only be used in combination with strings among the data types we have learned so far. We cannot use this function with numbers.

At the beginning, you remember that it was very important that we know what type of data we have at that moment, and that in Python we say that the type of data determines what you can and can't do with that data, right? Here len()is a very good example of this function.

len()function cannot be used with numbers. So if you don't know that the data you have is a number,len() can try to use in combination with the function, causing your program to crash and crash.

And as we said before, len() order to use the function correctly, we need to know that this function gives us a number-valued output.

len() After noting this situation aside about the function let's continue from where we left off.

Interactive Shell Memory

In the previous section, we have given some examples of how to use the interactive shell of Python, and have briefly introduced some of the basic tools of Python through the interactive shell. Now let's talk about another ability of Python's interactive shell.

In the interactive shell, the _ (underscore) serves to hold the value of the last operation or last item entered. So:

>>> 2345 + 54355

56700

If _we give the command after this process, we get an output like this:

>>> _

56700

As you can see, the _command keeps the last item entered in its memory. You can take advantage of this feature in several ways:

```
>>> _ + 15
```

56 715

Since the _value of the command is 56715 , which is the result of the previous operation , when we add 15 to the _command , we get the value of 56715 . Let's check the value of the command again: _

```
>>> _
```

56 715

As you can see, the _value of the command is now the number 56715...

_ command can store not only numbers, but also strings:

```
>>> "www"
```

'Www'

```
>>> _
```

'Www'

```
>>> _ + ".yazbel.com"
```

'Www.yazbel.co'

This sign is not a very common tool, but it makes your work quite easy from time to time. However, the only thing to remember is that this feature is only available in the interactive shell environment. _does not have any validity except the interactive shell environment.

Actually, there's more to say here. But for now, we'll leave them to the next issues. This is because our goal in this section is to warm you up to Python rather than to give you every detail.

print () Function

In the last chapter, while we are familiar with Python's interactive shell and learning some important functions and tools on this occasion, on the other hand, we have written sample programs by using this knowledge. As you can see, it is possible to write more or less useful programs with a little knowledge. There are many things we need to learn to write more useful programs. In this section, we will talk about a very important tool that will allow us to 'write more useful programs'. Because of its importance, we will explain in detail the name of this tool print().

Of course, this section will not only print()talk about the function. In this section print()we will cover some important basic issues in Python as well as function. In this section, for example, we will give some very important information about strings and numbers in Python. In addition print(), we have made a solid introduction to the topic of 'function' in Python on the occasion of its function, and will have our first knowledge of this concept. In essence, this section will be a turning point for us, if so, literally.

So print()let's start by explaining what the function is and what it does without further ado .

What is it?

So far, we have written both strings and numbers directly in the interactive shell. So we did something like:

>>> "Python programming language"

'Python programming language'

>>> 6567

6567

The interactive shell also outputed this string of characters and numbers directly to us. However, as you will see later when we save and run our Python code in a file, the above use is not enough for Python to output to the screen. So the above use only works in the interactive shell. When we try to save and run these codes in a file, we cannot get any output. In order to output what we write in Python, we print()need to use a special function called.

So print()let's try to understand what this function does and how it's used:

print()is a function just like we have seen before type(), len()and pow(). Remember, we said that we will examine the functions in more detail in the future. So don't let the things we talk about confuse you, disrupt your morale.

print()The function of the function is to provide output to the screen. Let's give an example:

>>> print ("Python programming language")

Python Programming Language

As you know, the "Python programming language burada we see here is a string. The print()function of this function is to output this string to the screen. But print()when we write this string without its function, do we not print it out? Actually, we're not. As we said, when you save and run our programs in the future, you will see print()that statements that are not at the beginning do not appear in the output.

As we said before, the interactive shell is a comfortable environment in terms of being a test environment. Therefore, you print()do not have to use the function to output the screen in this environment . So print() the interactive shell, whether it's at the beginning or not, prints what you want to print on the screen. But in terms of being a good habit, I print()recommend you to use the function when you print anything on the screen .

print()is an extremely powerful function. Let us take a deep look at this powerful and useful function.

How to use?

The first thing we notice in the above example is that we have print()written the string in parentheses of the function. We have learned in the last chapter that the elements specified in parentheses of a function are called 'parameters'. Just like the other functions we have learned, the print() function takes a number of parameters.

In the meantime print(), after opening the parenthesis of the function and writing the parameter, remember to close the parenthesis. One of the most common mistakes that beginners in the Python programming language, sometimes even experienced programmers, forgets to close the parentheses.

Of course, if we want to, instead of using the string "Python programming language doğrudan directly here, we can first assign it to a variable and then print()use it in parentheses. So:

>>> language = "Python programming language"

>>> print (language)

Python Programming Language

By the way, something must have caught your attention, both in the examples we have given and the examples we have written before. In the examples we have given so far, we have always shown strings with double quotes. But in fact, our only option is not double quotes. Python gives us three different quotes:

Single quotes ('')

Double quotes (" ")

Three quotes ("" "" "")

So we can write the above example in three different ways:

>>> print ('Python programming language')

Python programming language

>>> print ("Python programming language")

Python programming language

```
>>> print ( "" "Python programming language" "" )
```

Python programming language

As you can see, there is no difference between outputs.

If there is no difference in the output, why are there three different types of quotes?

Let's try to explain this question through an example. Let's say we want to give the screen an output like this:

The name of the Python programming language does not come from the "python" snake

If we show this sentence in double quotes, our program will give an error:

```
>>> print ( "Python programming language name does not come from" python "snake" )
```

File "<stdin>", line 1

  print ("Python programming language name does not come from" python "snake")

                        ^

SyntaxError: invalid syntax

The reason for this is that the word 'python' in the sentence is also shown in double quotes. Since the sentence itself, the string itself, is shown in double quotes, Python cannot distinguish between the quotes that start and end the string. We can easily print the above sentence in the following way:

>>> print ('Python programming language does not come from "python" snake')

The name of the Python programming language does not come from the "python" snake

Here we enclose the character string in single quotes. Since the word 'python' in the character string is in double quotes, it is not possible to mix the quotes that start and end the string with the quotes in the word 'python'.

Let's give an example: Let's say we want to get an output like the following:

Weather in Istanbul for 5 days

If you specify this string in single quotes, Python will display an error message:

```
>>> print ( 'Istanbul' s  5 -day  weather  condition  forecast ')
```

```
File "<stdin>", line 1
  print ('Istanbul's 5 day weather forecast')
              ^
```

SyntaxError: invalid syntax

The reason for this error is the apostrophe in the word 'Istanbul'. As in the previous example, Python cannot predict which quotes start and end the string. Python thinks that the string ends here when he sees the apostrophe in the word 'Istanbul' after the single quotation mark at the beginning of the string. But when he reads the string from left to right, he thinks there's something wrong and he has no choice but to show us an error message. We can easily define the above string as follows:

>>> print ("5-day weather forecast for Istanbul")

Weather in Istanbul for 5 days

Here, too, we enclose our character string in double quotation marks so that we do not get caught with the apostrophe in the string.

We can also use the three quotes to output the above strings properly:

>>> print ("" "Python programming language name does not come from" python "snake" "")

The name of the Python programming language does not come from the "python" snake

>>> print ("" "5 day weather forecast for Istanbul" "")

Weather in Istanbul for 5 days

After all these examples, you may have woken up in your mind:

Apparently, with three quotes, we are able to output any sequence of characters without error. Then you can better use three quotes for all the strings!

Of course, you can use three quotes for many strings if you want to. In Python, however, single quotes or double quotes are often used when defining strings. The actual use of the three quotes is different. What is the actual use of these three quotes?

Although we can use three quotation marks in combination with any string, this type of quotation is often used to define strings that span multiple lines. For example, imagine that you want to output a screen like this:

[H] HARMAN ========= ======== [-] [O] [x]

| |

| Welcome to the program! |

| Version 0.8 |

| Any |

| press a button. |

| |

| ================================= |

If you attempt to use single or double quotes to produce such output, you will suffer quite a bit. The easiest way to output this kind of output is to use three quotes:


```
>>> print ( """ "
... [H] ========== HARMAN ======== [-] [o] [x]
... | |
... | Welcome to the program! |
... | Version 0.8 |
... | any | to continue
... press | button. |
... | |
... | ============ ==================== |
... """ )
```

Things must have caught your attention here. As you can see, the three-tab structure behaves slightly differently than the other types of quotes. Now look at this example:

```
>>> print ( "" "Game Over!
...
```

Look here very carefully. After three nails character string to start, without putting the closing quotation Enter we press >>> mark ... it turned into a sign. In this way Python tells us, 'keep typing!' he says. Let's continue writing in accordance with this:

```
>>> print ( "" "Game Over!
... Insert Coin!" "" ))
```

Game Over!

Insert Coin!

When the Enter key is pressed before the closing tab is set , the >>> mark changes to the ... mark, which is unique to the three quotes. If you try to do the same with single or double quotes, your program will fail:

```
>>> print ( "Game Over!
```

```
File "<stdin>", line 1

  print ("Game Over!

        ^

SyntaxError: EOL while scanning string literal
```

...or:

```
>>> print ( 'Game Over!
```

```
File "<stdin>", line 1

  print ("Game Over!

        ^

SyntaxError: EOL while scanning string literal
```

This type of quotation is particularly suitable for displaying strings that span more than one line, thanks to the fact that the three quotation marks do not cause errors when the Enter key is pressed before the quotes close .

Let's give you another example of using three quotes:

```
>>> print ( """ "Python programming language by Guido Van
Rossum
... 90 named by a Dutch programmer
... has begun to develop at the beginning of the year. Most
of
... people, the name of the" Python "by looking at it, this
programming
.. . the language, think that takes its name from the
pythons.
... However, this programming language, in contrast to
what is generally assumed
... name does not come from python. """ " )
```

The Python programming language

was developed in the early 90s by a Dutch programmer
named

Guido Van Rossum . Most

people think that this programming

language derives its name from the python snake

, given the name "Python' . However, contrary to what is supposed, this programming language

does not come from the external python snake.

Of course, if we want, we can also choose to assign this text to a variable first:


```
>>> In python_hakk = "" "Python programming language by Guido Van Rossum
... 90 named by a Dutch programmer
... has begun to develop at the beginning of the year. Most
 ... people, the name of the" Python "by looking at it, this programming
.. The programming language thinks its name comes from the python snake
... However, contrary to the assumption, this programming language
... does not come from the python snake. "" "
>>> print ( python_hakkinda )
```

The Python Programming Language

This was developed in the early 90s by a Dutch programmer named Guido Van Rossum . Most people think that this programming language derives its name from the python snake, given the name "Python" . However, contrary to what is supposed, this programming language does not come from the external python snake. Think about how you can print the above output using single or double quotes, and we'll switch to an important topic!

Print () as a Function

print()If you recall that the expression is a function. As we said, we will give detailed explanations of functions in the following lessons. But now, if you wish, let's try to learn some basic things we need to know about functions so that we can better understand what we're going to say next.

As you can see, print()we use the function:

>>> print ("Type the word you want to search for:")

Here is print()a function, the string yazın Type the word you want to search for: ir is the parameter for this function. If you len()remember you have learned another function called before. We used it like this:

>>> len ("apple")

Here, too, len()a function and the apple character string are the parameters of this function. In fact , you can see that there is no difference between form print()and len()function.

As we said before and we can see from these examples, the elements specified in parentheses of a function are called parameters. For example, in the following example print(), we use the function with a single parameter:

>>> print ('Set at least 8-digit password.')

print()function, just like pow()function, can take multiple parameters:

>>> print ('Euphrates' , 'Specific')

Contact Fırat directly

In this example, there are many lessons to be learned for us. Once hereprint() function with two different parameters. The first is a series of characters called Fırat and the second is a series of characters called Özgül.

Note how Python combines these two strings. print()The function outputs these two strings and places a space between them. In addition, as we emphasized in the last lesson, we do not miss that the parameters are separated by commas.

Let us give you a few more examples about this:

>>> print ("Python" , "Programming" , "Language")

Python Programming Language

>>> print ('Fırat' , 'Özgül' , 'Adana' , 1980)

Contact Fırat directly

In the meantime, there is the need to draw your attention to an important point. In the examples above, we sometimes used single quotes and sometimes double quotes. As we said before, it doesn't matter which nail type we use. Python is more concerned with the consistency of quotes, rather than what type of quotes we use. So what's important for Python is that we should end the string with whatever quotation we started. So the following uses are not valid:

>>> print ("string")

>>> print ('string')

These two uses will fail because the quotation type used to define the character string and the type of quotation used to finish the character string are different.

Print () Function Parameters

The examples we have given so far may not be obvious, but actually print() function is an extremely powerful tool. Now, we will begin to examine the features of this function that reveal the power of this function. It is very important that you follow this section carefully so that you can understand the future works more easily.

SEP

print()When we examine the examples given above in relation to the function, we see that this function is a unique behavior. Let's look at the example we gave in the previous section:

>>> print ('Euphrates' , 'Specific')

Contact Fırat directly

Here we used the print()function with two different parameters. This function combined these parameters with each other in a certain order. In accordance with this scheme print(), when combining the given parameters, it places a space between the parameters. To see this more clearly, let's give another example:

>>> print ("Python" , "PHP" , "C ++" , "C" , "Erlang")

Python PHP C ++ C Erlang

As you can see, the print()function actually puts a space between each of the parameters when combining the given parameters. However, we did not demand this gap! Python gave us this space as a giveaway. In most cases this is what we want, but in some cases we may not want this gap. For example:

>>> print ("http: //" , "www." , "recruitment." , "com")

http: // www. sarcasm. com

Or we may want to use a different character instead of a space character. So what should we do in such a situation?

At this point, taking advantage of some special tools print() make changes to the default behavior patterns of the function.

What print()are these tools that allow us to customize the function?

If you remember, we said that the values in parentheses in Python are called parameters. For example print(), we know that we can use the function with one or more parameters:

>>> print ("Mehmet" , "Abstract" , "Istanbul" , "Camlica" , 156 , "/" , 45)

More professionals named Mehmet Oz Camlica

print() We can use any number of character strings and / or number-valued parameters within the function.

The functions also have more specific looking parameters. For example, the print()function has a special parameter called sep . This parameter print()is always there even if it does not appear in the function. So let's say we wrote code like this:

>>> print ("http: //" , "www." , "google." , "com")

We don't see any sep parameters here . But Python actually detects the above code like this:

```
>>> print ( "http: //" , "www." , "google." , "com" , sep = "" )
```

sep is the abbreviation of separator in English . Therefore, print()this sep parameter in the function indicates which character is to be placed among the items to be printed on the screen. The default value of this parameter is a space character (we "). So if you don't replace the value of this special parameter with something else, Python will take the value of this parameter as a space character and separate the items to be printed with a space. But if we want this sepWe can change the value of parameter. Thus, when combining strings, Python can insert any other character we want, not spaces. Now let's see how we change the value of this parameter:

```
>>> print ( "http: //" , "www." , "recruitment." , "com" , sep = "" )
```

I http://www.istihza.co

As you can see, we've successfully combined strings to get a valid internet address.

What we're doing here is actually very simple. We just deleted the default value of the sep parameter, which is 'one space character', and replaced it with 'empty string'. You remember we said these two concepts were different, right?

Let's make another example:

```
>>> print ( "T" , "C" , sep = "." )
```

TC

Here we have given Python an order:

Combine "T" and "C" strings! While doing this, place a period between these strings!

The difference of the sep parameter from the other parameters is that it is always used with its name. Already technically, such parameters are called 'named parameters'. For example:

```
>>> print ( "Adana" , "Mersin" , sep = "-" )
```

Adana-Mersin

If we write here directly the value of the parameter without specifying the name of the sep parameter, this value will be no different from the other parameters:

```
>>> print ( "Adana" , "Mersin" , "-" )
```

Adana Mersin -

Let's make another example about this parameter:

'One candle is two candles ...' he began to know the folk song. Now let's see how we can write this with Python!

```
>>> print ( "one" , "two" , "three" , "four" , "fourteen" ,
sep = "candle" )
```

amultiportimummaximumthreecurrentfour fourtold four

It's clear there's something wrong here! Strings are joined together in a cramped order. It would be better if there was a gap between them. However, you know that because we deleted the default value of the sep parameter and replaced it with "candle", Python's automatic space character disappeared. But if we want, we can also set those space characters ourselves:

```
>>> print ( "one" , "two" , "three" , "four" , "fourteen" ,
sep = "candle" )
```

one candle two candle three candle four candle fourteen

As you can see, we were able to solve our problem by leaving a space to the left and right of the "candle" value we gave to the sep parameter. There is another way to solve this problem. If you remember, we said that we can also use the + sign to join strings in the interactive shell. So we can also write the sep parameter:

```
>>> print ( "one" , "two" , "three" , "four" , "fourteen' ,
sep = "" + "is the candle" + "" )
```

Here, instead of leaving a space at the beginning and erd of the string dur mumdur " , we put the required spaces into the string with the help of the + sign. You even know that we don't have to use the + operator if we want to:

```
>>> print ( "one" , "two" , "three" , "four" , "fourteen" ,
sep = "" "is the candle" "" )
```

But as you can see, we have another problem. The lyrics of the Turks should be as follows:

one candle two candle three candle four candle fourteen candle

But the word 'candle' at tne end does not appear in the above output. That's normal, actually. The sep parameter places a value between strings. It does not deal with the last side of strings. The print()function for this job has another parameter.

In the meantime, don't be fooled that we have always used strings in the examples above. The sep parameter can place a desired value between not only strings but also numbers. E.g:

>>> print (1 , 2 , 3 , 4 , 5 , sep = "-")

1-2-3-4-5

However, we can only supply strings and a special word called None as the sep parameter . (None will be mentioned later):

>>> print (1 , 2 , 3 , 4 , 5 , sep = 0)

Traceback (most recent call last):

  File "<stdin>" , line 1 , in <module>

TypeError : sep

As you can see, we cannot give the sep parameter a value of 0 .

What if we set this parameter to None ? When this parameter is set to None , the print()function uses the default value (that is, a space) for this parameter:

>>> print ('a' , 'b' , sep = None)

ab

If your goal is to one another concatenate parameters, namely SEP parameters of the character is to eliminate the gap, which is the default value, SEP , you know you must provide a parameter to an empty string:

>>> print ('a' , 'b' , sep = '')

ab

print()Since we have examined the sep parameter in all details, we can talk about another special parameter of this function.

end

In the previous section, we said:

print()The function has a special parameter called sep . This parameter print()is always there even if it does not appear in the function.

In the same way, the print()function has a special parameter called end . Just like the sep parameter, the end parameter print() is always there, even if it does not appear in its function.

As you know, the parameters given to the sep parameter print()function determine which characters to insert when joining. The end parameter determines what will come to the end of these parameters.

print()function adds 'carriage return' to the end of the parameters by default. So what's this carriage return character (or 'newline character')?

Let's see this on an example.

Let's have a code like this:

>>> print ("Pardus and Ubuntu are GNU / Linux distributions.")

As soon as we enter this code and press Enter , the print()function performs two different operations:

Prints the string of characters on the screen first.

Then move to the bottom line and show us the >>> sign.

This second operation is print()caused by the fact that the function has a carriage return character at the end of the string, or rather the function adds the carriage return character to the end of the string. This statement may have been a bit confusing. Then let's explain more. See example:

>>> print ("Pardus \ n Ubuntu")

Pardus

Ubuntu

Here you can see another very special string in the middle of the "Pardus" and "Ubuntu" strings. This string is: \ n . This special string is called newline. The task of this character is to divide the string from its current position and move the rest of the string to a bottom line. You already see that it performs this function in the output. The string is split into two after the "Pardus" section, and the rest of the string "Ubuntu" is printed on a bottom line. Here's another example to better understand this:

```
>>> print ( "first line \ n second line \ n third line" )
```

first line

second line

third line

Let me ask you a question: How can we write the above codes more efficiently?

Yes, you've guessed correctly ... Of course using the sep parameter:

```
>>> print ( "first line" , "second line" , "third line" , sep = "
\ n " )
```

first line

second line

third line

What we do here is very simple. We changed the value of the sep parameter to \ n , which is the newline character (or carriage return character). Thus , we placed \ n characters between strings so that each string could be printed on different lines.

The default value of the end parameter is this \ n character and print()is always there, even if it does not appear in this parameter function.

So let's say we wrote code like this:

```
>>> print ( "Today is Tuesday" )
```

We don't see any end parameters here . But Python actually detects the above code like this:

>>> print ("Today is Tuesday" , end = " \ n ")

As we said before, when we type this code and press Enter , the print()function performs two different operations:

Prints the string of characters on the screen first.

Then move to the bottom line and show us the >>> sign.

To understand what this means, simply change the value of the end parameter:

>>> print ("Today is Tuesday" , end = ".")

Today is Tuesday. >>>

As you can see, delete \ n, which is the default value of the end parameter. (dot), we did not pass the function to the beginning of the line when we type the command and press Enter . To enter the new line , we have to press Enter . Of course, if you type the code above, the function will add a period to the end of the string and pass to the beginning of the line:print()print()

```
>>> print ( "Today is Tuesday" , end = ". \ n " )
```

Today is Tuesday.

Now let's apply what we have learned to our Turkish:

```
>>> print ( "one" , "two" , "three" , "four" , "fourteen" ,

... sep = "is candle" , end = "is candle \ n " )
```

In order to prevent the ugly extension of our codes to the right, we entered the "fourteen" string of characters and put a comma, then we entered the bottom line by pressing Enter . When we get to a bottom line >>> the mark ... Notice how the mark. As well as writing the correct code in Python, it is important that the code we write looks good. So we must ensure that each line of code we write does not exceed 79 characters as much as possible. If a line you type exceeds 79 characters, you can move the surplus to the bottom line as shown above.

The end parameter, like the sep parameter, is a parameter that should always be used with its name. So if we try to use only the value of the end parameter without specifying the name, Python cannot understand what we are trying to do.

Just like the sep parameter, the value of the end parameter can be just one string or None :

```
>>> print ( 1 , 2 , 3 , 4 , 5 , end = 0 )
```

```
Traceback (most recent call last):
  File "<stdin>" , line 1 , in <module>
TypeError : None or a string, not int
```

As you can see, we cannot give the end parameter a value of 0 .

If we set this parameter to None, the function uses the default value (ie the carriage return character) for this parameter, as in the sep parameter print():

```
>>> print ( 'a' , 'b' , end = None )
```

ab

If your goal is to prevent the introduction of the new line, that end with a default value of the parameter \ n is to eliminate the escape sequence, end should give an empty string parameter:

```
>>> print ( 'a' , 'b' , end = '' )
```

a b >>>

file

Here are some things we haven't learned yet. Don't worry at all. We will learn them in detail in the future. For now, if we can get some idea about the subject, we will consider ourselves successful.

print()function of sep and a third custom parameter other than end . The name of this parameter is file. Its print() function is to specify the string and / or numbers given to the function, where the parameters are to be written.

The default value of this parameter sys.stdout . Well what does it mean? sys.stdout means 'standard output position'. What does 'standard output position' mean?

Standard output position; This is where a program produces its output. In fact, it is understood from the name:

standard output position = the position where the outputs are delivered as standard.

For example, Python defaults to the output it produces. If you are currently working in the interactive shell, Python shows the output it produces on the interactive shell. If you run a program you are writing on the command line, the generated output appears on the command line. Therefore, Python's standard output location is the interactive shell or command line. This means print()that the output you print with the help function will appear in the interactive shell or command line.

Now let's make a few examples to better understand this issue.

Under normal circumstances print()we see the output of the function in the interactive shell:

>>> print ("I'm Python, Monty Python!")

I'm Python, Monty Python!

But if we want print(), we can have the function print its output to a file, not the screen. For example, we now print() function , let's output the to a file named test.txt .

To do this, let's write the following codes:

>>> file = open ("trial.txt" , "w")

>>> print ("I'm Python, Monty Python!" , file = file)

>>> file . close ()

You didn't get any printout, did you? Yeah. Because of these codes we wrote the print()function, the output to a file called trial.txt .

Let us examine the above codes line by line:

1. First, we created a file named test.txt and assigned it to a variable named file. Don't get open()too attached to the function we use here . We will examine this in a few chapters. Let us know that the file is created in this way for now. Meanwhile, openthe function of the form as type(), len(), pow()and print()note that how similar their functions. As you can see open()in function just as type(), len(), pow()and print()is taking a number of parameters such functions. The first parameter of this function is a string called "test.txt .. This string represents the name of the file we want to create. The second parameter isAnother string of characters named "w .. This means that the trial.txt file will open in write mode (mode). But as said, don't worry about these details for now. In the following lessons, you can be sure that you know these topics as if you know your name.

2. This file named trial.txt that we created will be created in the current directory. To find out which directory this is, you can issue the following commands:

```
>>> import os
```

>>> os . getcwd ()

Which directory name appears in the output of this command, the trial.txt file is also in that directory. For example, I have output / home / yazbel / Desktop . Which means that the file trial.txt which was created was on the desktop? I gave these commands on Ubuntu. If I gave it on Windows I would get a printout similar to: C: \ Users \ yazbel \ Desktop

3. Then we print()ran our function normally . But as you can see the print()function did not give us any output. Because, as print()we said before, we set the function to output to the file, not the screen. This process, file a parameter, called a little while ago we define file 've done typing the variable.

4. With the help of the last command, we close the file we opened in order to make the changes appear in the file.

Now open the file named trial.txt . You 'll see that the string "I'm Python, Monty Python!", Whichprint() we just printed with the function , is orocessed into the file.

Thus print(), we have changed the standard output position of the function. That print()is , by giving a different value to the parameter named file ,print() we provide interactive writing not to shell the function file.

Just like the sep and end parameters, the file parameter is always in the print()function even if you don't see it . So let's say we have a command like this:

>>> print ("It's not a shame to be Tahir" or "To be a pooh")

Python detects this command:

>>> print ("It's not a shame either" , "It is not a shame " ,

... sep = "" , end = " \ n " , file = sys . stdout)

In other words, when printing the values given as parameters to the screen, it performs the following operations respectively:

Puts a space between the parameters ( ),sep=" "

Appends a carriage return to the end of the parameters after printing (end="\n")

Sends this output to the standard output position (file=sys.stdout).

Here is where we file value of the parameter by giving another value to the standard output location.

Let's make another example. For example, let's save our personal information in a file. First of all, let's create the file where we will save the information:

```
>>> f = open ( "personal_information.txt" , "w" )
```

With these codes, we opened a file named personal_info.txt in write mode (w) and assigned it to a variable named f . Now we can start writing the information:

```
>>> print ( "Firat Ozgul" , file = f )
>>> print ( "Adana" , file = f )
>>> print ( "Ubuntu" , file = f )
```

When we're done, we don't forget to close the file. So all the information is written to the file:

>>> f . close ()

When we open the file named personal_information.txt , we print() see that the parameters we give to the function are printed to the file.

As said at the beginning, in this section, we came across some things that we haven't learned yet. If you have difficulty understanding the examples given above, you don't have to worry. After a few chapters, what we're talking about here will sound like a piece of cake to you...

flush

So far we have learned that the print()function has some special parameters called sep , end and file . print()The function has another special parameter. The name of this parameter is flush. Now we will talk about print()this flush parameter of the function .

As you know, when print()we issue a command such as, Python sends the information we want to print to the standard output location. However, in Python, some processes are buffered for a while before being sent to the standard output location, and then those pending processes are sent to the standard output location collectively. So what does this statement, which at first seems to be very complicated?

In fact, you are no stranger to this phenomenon. Consider the following example when describing the file parameter:

>>> f = open ("personal_information.txt" , "w")

With this command, we opened a file named personal_info.txt in write mode. Now let's add some information to this file:

>>> print ("Fırat Özgül" , f le = f)

With this command, we added a line called 'Fırat Özgül' to the file named personal_bilgiler.txt .

Now open this personal_information.txt file that occurs on your computer. As you can see, there is no information in the file. The file currently appears to be empty. However, we just added a line called 'Fırat Özgül' to this file, didn't we?

Python has saved the line we want to add to this file. When file write operations ended Python, all waiting position information to the standard output buffer (ie, in our case, for it holds the variable named kişisel_bilgiler.txt file named) will be empty.

Let's write more information in the file:

```
>>> print ( "Adana" , file = f )
>>> print ( "Ubuntu" , file = f )
```

That's all we're gonna put in the file. We now issue the following command to notify Python that the write process has ended:

```
>>> f . close ()
```

So we closed our file. Now double-click the file named personal_information.txt to open it again. There you will see 'Fırat Özgül', 'Adana' and 'Ubuntu'.

As you can see, Python actually kept all the data we want to write to the file in the buffer first, and then emptied all the data that was waiting in the buffer when the file was closed. With the flush parameter, you can control this unloading process. Now carefully review:

>>> f = open ("personal_information.txt" , "w")

We created our file. Now let's add some information to this file:

>>> print ("Hello World!" , file = f , flush = True)

As you can see, we used a new parameter called flush here. The value we give to this parameter is True. Now double-click the file to open it. As you can see, the information was written to the file even though we did not close the file yet. This is because, as you can imagine, we set the flush parameter to True. This parameter can take two values: True and False. The default value of this parameter is False. This means that if we do not specify any value for this parameter, Python will accept the value of this parameter as False and wait for the file to close for the information to be written to the file. However, this parameter When set to true, the data will be sent to the standard output position without waiting in the buffer.

In a program you write, you may want the information you want to write to a file to be stored in the buffer for a while or to be written directly to the file without waiting, depending on the nature of the job you want to do. You can also set the value of the flush parameter to True or False, depending on your needs.

A Few Practical Information

Until we came here, we print()talked a lot about the function and its parameters. Now, if you wish, let us give you some tips that will help you in your programming adventure.

Starred Parameters

Now let's ask you a question: How do we get an output like this?

La . [0132] i . [0135] n .u . x

You might immediately have an answer:

>>> print ("L" , "i" , "n" , "u" , "x" , sep = ".")

Linux

The above is indeed the right solution. But there is a much simpler way to solve this question. Now look carefully:

>>> print (* "Linux" , sep = ".")

Linux

Before moving on to the topic, let's give you another example:

>>> print (* "Galatasaray")

G alatasaray

It's more or less guessing what's going on here. As you can see in the last example, the "Galatasaray" character we added to the beginning of the asterisk; "Galatasaray ayır breaks down each element of the string and print()sends it to its individual function. So it's as if print()we wrote the function:

>>> print ("G" , "a" , "l" , "a" , "t" , "a" , "s" , "a" , "r" , "a" , "y")

G alatasaray

As said, the asterisk that we add at the beginning of a string that we give as a parameter to a function, naturally separates this character string into individual elements, and sends these elements to that function as if each element is a separate parameter, but naturally more than one asterisk we can apply it to functions that can take parameters.

For example, the len()function can only take one parameter:

>>> len ("Galatasaray")

11th

We cannot use this function with more than one parameter:

```
>>> len ( "Galatasaray" , "Fenerbahce" , "Besiktas" )
```

Traceback (most recent call last):

  File "<stdin>" , line 1 , in <module>

TypeError : len () takes exactly one argument (3 given)

As stated in the error message, the len()function can only take a single parameter, we 3 tried to give parameters ...

So we len()can't apply starred parameters to the function:

```
>>> len ( * "Galatasaray" )
```

Traceback (most recent call last):

  File "<stdin>" , line 1 , in <module>

TypeError : len () takes exactly one argument (11 given)

When we add a star to the beginning of a parameter, it is as if we have given 11 different parameters to the en()function instead of 1, since all the elements that make up that parameter are sent to the individual function.

In order to apply starred parameters to a function, the structure of that function must be suitable for taking starred parameters as well as taking more than one parameter. For example open(), type()and the len()structure of the functions we mentioned earlier is not suitable for taking the star parameter. Therefore, we cannot use starred parameters with every function, but print()it is a very convenient function for starred parameters:

>>> print (* "Galatasaray")

G alatasaray

>>> print (* "TGNA" , sep = ".")

Turkish Grand National Assembly

>>> print (* "abcdefdef" , sep = "/")

a / b / c / c / d / e / f / g / g / h

As you can see from these examples, when print()we add a star to the beginning of a parameter to the print()function, it is seperated and sent to the function. parameter is applied to the string elements one by one because .

Remember that the default value of the sep parameter is a space character. So actually Python sees the first command above:

>>> print (* "Galatasaray" , sep = "")

Therefore, thanks to the asterisk, a space character is placed between each element of the series "Galatasaray karakter. In the next "TBMM" character string, a dot is placed between each element of the "TBMM" character string because we change the value of the sep parameter to a period. Likewise, by sending each element of the string "abcçdefgğh una to its individual function, we can place this / sign between each element with the / sign given to the sep parameter .print()

The only limitation for starred parameters is that they cannot be used with numbers:

>>> print (* 2345)

Traceback (most recent call last):

  File "<stdin>" , line 1 , in <module>

TypeError : print () argument after * must be a sequence, not int

Because starred parameters can only be used in combination with data types that have array properties. For example, strings are a data type of this type. In the following, we will learn about other types of data that can be used in conjunction with the starred parameters.

The examples above show us that star parameters are very useful tools. In the future, we will benefit abundantly from these parameters. Now let's close this matter here and talk about something else.

Permanently Changing sys.stdout

As you can see from the examples given in the previous headings, we can temporarily change the standard output position of Python using the file parameter of the print() function . But in some cases, you may want to specify a non-standard output location for programs that you write during the program's operation. This means that you may need to change the standard output position permanently, not temporarily. For example, in the program you write, you can choose to print all the output to a file. Of course, you can do this each time by setting the file parameter to the name of the file you want to print out. Just as in the following example:

```
>>> f = open ( "file.txt" , "w" )
>>> print ( "Firat Ozgul" , file = f )
>>> print ( "Adana" , file = f )
>>> print ( " Ubuntu " , file = f )
>>> f . close ()
```

As you can see, we've done the job by giving the value of f to the file parameter each time. But there is a more practical way of doing this. If you wish, you can redirect the output to another location during the entire operation of the program you are writing. For this, we will use some information that we have already learned and which we have not yet learned.

First, let's write a code like this:

```
>>> import  sys
```

With the help of this code, we have included a special 'module' called sys in our program. What is a 'module', what does 'import' mean?

In fact, we are not alien to these concepts of 'module' and 'import'. In the previous lessons, we have already met a few modules in Python, though we did not dwell on them. For example, using a function inside a module called os , we getcwd()were able to find out which directory we're currently in:

```
>>> import  os
>>> os . getcwd ()
```

In the same way, we were able to list which words cannot be used as a variable name in Python by using the variable kwlist in another module called keyword:

```
>>> import  keyword
>>> keyword . kwlist
```

Now we're talking about a module called sys in addition to the os and keyword modules. Let us leave the other modules aside for now and let us pay attention to this module called sys.

As we said, there are many important variables and functions in the sys module. However, in order to use variables and functions within a module, we first need to include that module in our program, that is, import it. We importdo this with the command:

>>> import sys

We will now be able to access all functions and variables within the sys module.

One of the many variables and functions in the sys module is stdout . You can access the value of this variable as follows:

>>> sys . stdout

This command outputs something similar to:

< _io . TextIOWrapper   name = '<stdout>'   mode = 'w' encoding = 'cp1254' >

Note the name = '<stdout>' in this output . We'il get back to this statement soon. Now let's talk about something else.

If you remember how to turn off the interactive shell, we said that one way to get out of the interactive shell is to give the following commands:

>>> import sys ; sys . exit ()

We wrote this command on a single line, but we could also write it if we wanted:

>>> import sys

>>> sys . exit ()

As we said, there are many variables and functions in the sys module. How stdout is one of the variables within the sys module is exit()also one of the functions contained in the sys module.

We will examine the 'modules' in detail in the following lessons. For the time being, let's only know about the modules:

1. In Python, modules importare imported with the command. For example , we command to import the module named sys .import sys

2. There are many useful variables and functions within the modules. When we import a module, we have the opportunity to use these variables and functions within that module.

3. sys An example of variables in the module is stdout ; An example of a exit()function is the function. These variables and functions within a module can be accessed   us ng   the   formula 'module_name.variable_da_da_function'.   For example:

>>> sys . stdout

>>> sys .exit ()

4. If you remember, before we open()explained how to create a file with the function, we used the following codes to identify the current directory in order to find out which directory the file is in:

```
>>> import os
>>> os . getcwd()
```

Here we see another module called os . So os is a module just like sys , and just like in sys , there are many useful variables and functions inside the os module. getcwd()The function named is a function in the os module that shows which directory we are currently in. Of course, just like in the sys module, os also useful to be able to use these variables and functions within this module primarily os we import the module, so we need to incorporate into our program. os moduleimportAfter the proper import via the command, getcwd()we can access the function named in the module again using the formula 'module_name.function'.

Enough information about the modules for now. Let's put the modules aside and move on ...

If sys.exit()you commanded and exited the interactive shell, re-enter the interactive shell and re-import the sys module:

>>> import sys

Simply import a module once in the same interactive shell session. Once you import a module, you can continue to use variables and functions within that module during that session. But, of course, after you close the interactive shell and turn it back on, you must re-import a module to use it.

Now type the following code:

>>> f = open ("file.txt" , "w")

You know the meaning of this code. Here we opened a file named file.txt in write mode. As you can imagine, we will redirect our output to this file instead of the screen.

Now let's write a code like this:

>>> sys . stdout = f

As you know, the value of sys.stdout determines where Python outputs the output. Here we are replacing the value of sys.stdout with the file f we just created . So Python sends all the output to the file named file.txt , which we specified in the variable f .

From now on, everything you type will go to file.txt :

>>> print ("test text" , flush = True)

As you can see, although we did not use the file parameter here, our output was printed on a file named file.txt , not the screen . But how did this happen? Well, the answer to this is very simple: a little while ago with the command sys.stdout 's value for 've changed files kept by the variable. Before you do thissys.stdout = fsys.stdout remember that the value of is:

< _io . TextIOWrapper   name = '<stdout>'   mode= 'w' encoding = 'cp1254' >

but sys.stdout = f after the command everything changed. Let's check:

>>> print (sys . stdout , flush = True)

Of course, you didn't get any printouts from this command. Open the file named file.txt to see what the output is . There you will see the following line:

< _io . TextIOWrapper   name = 'file.txt'   mode = 'w' encoding = 'cp1254' >

As you can see, the original name = '<stdout>' in the stdout output was name = 'file.txt . So now all the output goes to the file named file.txt ...

By the way, the above output name , mode, and encoding you can access values that follows:

>>> sys . stdout . name

>>> sys . stdout . mode

>>> sys .stdout . encoding

Here the sys.stdout.namecommand will give the current name   of   the   standard   output   location. sys.stdout.modeindicates which mode the standard output position has. The standard output position is usually found in write mode (w).sys.stdout.encodingcode indicates the encoding format of the standard output location. The

197

encoding format determines which encoding format the characters you print to the standard output location are encoded. The encoding format is usually 'cp1254' on Windows and 'utf-8' on GNU / Linux. If this encoding format is incorrect, for example, the Turkish letters in the characters you write to the file cannot be displayed properly. If what we say here does not seem to be understandable to you right now, you can continue on your way without taking into account what we have said. After a few chapters this will begin to mean more to you than what we say anyway.

What if you want to restore the standard output position? You can exit the interactive shell and re-enter it. When you reopen the interactive shell, you will see that everything is restored. Likewise, if you had written these codes into a program file, everything would be restored when your program closed.

Is there a way to restore the standard output location without exiting the interactive shell or closing the program? Of course there is. Look carefully:

```
>>> import sys
```

```
>>> f = open ( "file.txt" , "w" )

>>> sys . stdout , f = f , sys . stdout

>>> print ( "test" , flush = True )

>>> f , sys . stdout = sys . stdout , f

>>> print ( "trial" )
```

trial

If you are unable to run the above code, the code you previously provided in the same interactive shell session may be preventing it from output correctly. To overcome this problem, turn the interactive shell off and on again, and run the above commands again.

Actually, there's nothing you can't understand here. We did what we did here in the last chapters, explaining how to trade the value of variables. Let us remember:

```
>>> osman = "Research and Development Manager"

>>> mehmet = "Project Officer"

>>> osman , mehmet = mehmet , osman
```

With these codes, we exchanged the titles of Osman and Mehmet. That's what we've done above. when we say f is sys.stdout , and sys.stdout is fsys.stdout, f = f, sys.stdout given to . When we say, by doing the opposite of this process, we have restored everything.f, sys.stdout = sys.stdout, f

Taking advantage of Python's ease of use, we can easily exchange the value of variables. If this was not the case, we could have written the above code:

```
>>> import  sys
>>> f  =  open ( "file.txt" ,  "w" )
>>> original_stdout  =  sys . stdout
>>> sys . stdout  =  f
>>> print ( "test" ,  flush = True )
>>> sys . stdout  =  original_stdout
>>> print ( "experiment" )
```

trial

As you can see, sys.stdout 's to lose its value, sys.stdout value f them towing the help of these codes before sending the file named:


```
>>> original_stdout = sys . stdout
```

Since we have assigned the original value of sys.stdout to the original_stdout variable, we will be able to reach it again later. As you can already see from the above code, sys.stdout we want to return to the original value of we can execute the request by typing the following code:


```
>>> sys . stdout = original_stdout
```

thus stdout value is restored, and everything we print is now reprinted.

... and so we left a long section behind. In this section print() , we have examined the function in detail, as well as other very important concepts about Python programming language. So this part has taught us a lot. Now that we have learned this information by putting our head on the way we can continue to stand upright.

Expert's Guide: Advanced, To Expert Concepts

Installation Guide

Installing Fedora 12 on x86, AMD64, and Intel 64 systems

Revision 1.0

This guide uses different styles to highlight text.

The same fonts will be used to display the HTML version if they are installed on your system. Otherwise, similar fonts will be used. Red Hat Enterprise Linux 5 and later versions include a default Liberation kit.

Typographical conventions

Four styles are used to select text, which will be listed below.

Monospaced bold

Used to highlight typed text, including shell commands, as well as file names, paths, and shortcut keys. Example:

To view the contents of a file my_next_bestselling_novelin the current directory, at the shell prompt, type cat my_next_bestselling_noveland press Enter to execute this command.

The text contains the file name, the shell command, and the key name, which are in monospaced bold type.

A hyphen is used to separate keys as part of a combination. Example:

Press Enter to execute the command.

Press Ctrl + Alt + F1 to go to the first virtual terminal. Press Ctrl + Alt + F7 to return to the X-Windows session.

In the first example, the name of a single key is highlighted in bold, in the second - key combinations.

The same font distinguishes the names of classes, methods, functions, variables and the values returned by them. Example:

File classes include filesystemfor file systems, filefor files, dirfor directories. Each class corresponds to a set of permissions.

Proportional fat

Highlights system words and phrases, which include application names, dialog text, menu names, text for buttons, checkboxes, and other GUI elements. Example:

In the main menu, select System → Settings → Mouse to launch the Mouse Settings utility. On the Buttons tab, select the Adjust mouse under left hand checkbox and click the Close button to configure the mouse for left-handed users.

To insert a special character in the gedit file, select Applications → Accessories → Character Table. Then select Search → Search... from the menu, enter a symbol name and click the Find Next button. The found character will be highlighted in the symbol table. Double-click on this symbol to paste it into the Text to copy field and click Copy. Now go back to your document and select Edit → Paste from the menu.

The text above contains the name of the application, the names of the menus, buttons, and text of the GUI elements.

Monospace bold italic or proportional bold italic

Both types of selection denote changeable or replaceable text. Italics indicate that you should not enter the text directly, but change it according to your settings. Example:

To connect to a remote machine using SSH at the prompt, execute. Say the name of the remote computer - and your user name - john, then the command would look like this:. ssh

username@domain_nameexample.comssh john@example.com

The command reconnects the specified file system. For example, it would look like the command:. mount -o remount filesystem / homemount -o remount / home

To view the version of the installed package, run the command. Will be presented in the format. rpm -q package-version-release

In the examples above, the user name, domain name, file system, package, version, and release are highlighted in bold italics.

Also italicized terms that appear in the text of the document for the first time. Example:

Publican - DocBook publishing system .

Text selection conventions

Screenshot of the surrounding text.

To use the monospaced font:

```
books desktop documentation drafts mss photos stuff svn
books_tests Desktop1 downloads images notes scripts svgs
```

To display the contents of the source code is used monospace font:

```
package org. jboss . book . jca . exl ;

import javax.naming.InitialContext;

publ┌─────────────────────────────────┐
{   │ 1.2. Text selection conventions │
    └─────────────────────────────────┘
    public  static  void  main (String args [])
         throws Exception
    {
       InitialContext iniCtx = new InitialContext ();
       Object ref = iniCtx. lookup ( "EchoBean" );
       EchoHome home = (EchoHome) ref;
       Echo echo = home. create ();

       System. out . println ( "Created Echo" );

       System. out . println ( "Echo.echo ('Hello') =" + echo. echo ( "Hello" ));
    }
}
```

Notes and warnings

Finally, three styles are used to draw the reader's attention to important information.

Note

Notes usually contain additional information. If you ignore them, this is not critical, but you can skip the tip, which may help save time during the assignment.

Important

It will be easy to use it. Ignoring a box labeled "Important" and no data loss.

A warning

Do not ignore the warnings, as they contain important information that will avoid data loss.

We need your feedback!

This guide covers installing Fedora, a Linux distribution based on open source and free software. You will learn how to install Fedora on workstations, laptops and servers. The structure of the installation process is quite simple, even for novice Linux users. Basically, you can choose standard settings and install the standard Fedora suite, which includes Internet utilities, desktop tools, and performance applications.

This is a list of installation options, including those that apply only in limited or limited circumstances. The Fedora 12 is a quick installation guide for you. The Fedora 12 Installation Quick Start Guide is available from

http://docs.fedoraproject.org/installation-quick-start-guide/ .

About Fedora

To find out more about Fedora, refer to http://fedoraproject.org/ . Related topics, refer to http://docs.fedoraproject.org/ .

Getting help

For information on additional help resources for Fedora, visit http://fedoraproject.org/wiki/Communicate .

File upload

Do one of the following:

Check downloaded files

Always check the sha256sum downloaded files.

Download the Live ISO image and burn it to disk. The livecd-tools package allows you to write an image to another type of bootable media, such as USB. To start the installation on the hard disk, after logging in, click on the corresponding icon on the desktop.

Download the ISO images of the full distribution and burn them to a CD or DVD, or place the images in a Windows FAT32 or Linux ext2 / ext3 partition.

Download the image boot.isofor a minimum bootable CD or USB and burn it to the appropriate media. It will not contain packages and must point to a local or remote repository with packages.

Download a netinst.isoreduced-size bootable CD.

Download the vmlinuzkernel file initrd.imgfrom the distribution isolinux / directory. The ramdisk image. For further information on installation, installation without media.

If you can install Fedora, refer to Chapter 10, Setting Up the Installation Server.

To learn how to turn ISO images into CD or DVD media, refer to http://docs.fedoraproject.org/readme-burning-isos/ .

Preparing to install

Back up any data you want to back up.

Resizing partitions

The installation program provides functions for resizing ext2, ext3, ext4, and NTFS formatted partitions. Refer to Section 6.21, "Partitioning a Disk" for more information.

Installing Fedora

Options for your hardware and installation mode, boot Options for more information about boot options. If you boot from the Live CD, select the "Install to Hard Disk" option. If you boot from the network, choose a network or hard disk resource from which to install.

Continue the installation. The installation program does not make any major changes to the system until you confirm the continuation of the installation. When finished, reboot the system.

Post-install steps

After the system reboots, you will be prompted to configure additional settings, after which the login screen will appear.

Refer to Chapter 14, Firstboot or the Firstboot page on the Fedora wiki: http://fedoraproject.org/wiki/FirstBoot for more detail.

Getting Fedora

Getting Fedora on CD / DVD

Understand and run Fedora on your computer. If you have an operating system. If you have any questions about th`s topic, go to http://www.fedoraforum.org/ .

The Fedora Project provides many ways to get a distribution, mostly free and open to download. The most common installation method is using a CD or DVD, including:

Full set of programs on DVD

Live images that you can use to get familiar with Fedora, and then install it if you like Fedora

Boot images of CDs and small USB drives that can be used to install Fedora over the network

DVD source code

Usually, users prefer to resort to using Live images or full sets of CD / DVD. Shortened boot images are suitable for installing Fedora on one computer if you have a fast Internet connection. Source code drives are not used to install Fedora, but serve only as a source of code for experienced users and programmers.

Users with broadband Internet access can download ISO images of CD / DVDs or USB drives. An ISO image is a copy of a complete disc in a format sufficient for direct recording onto a CD or DVD. USB image - copy, ready to write to a flash drive.

CDs and DVDs, refer to Section 2.1.4, "How can I create Fedora installation media?" .

If you're referring to Section "Getting Fedora on CD / DVD" .

Fedora boot

How to download the installation files?

Download links

To follow a Web-based guide to downloading, visit http://get.fedoraproject.org/ . Refer to Section 2.1.2, "How to find out the architecture of my computer?" .

Fedora software is available for free download. Ways:

Mirror

The Fedora installation files are freely available from web servers located in many parts of the world. These servers mirror the files available from the Fedora Project. If you visit http://download.fedoraproject.org/ , you are redirected to a mirror. Alternatively, you can choose a mirror from the list maintained at http://mirrors.fedoraproject.org/publiclist. This page lists mirrors according to geographic location. The mirrors are geographically closest to downloads. If you are a mirror or organization, it will be a mirror.

The hierarchy of Fedora software files on mirror servers is organized quite effectively. For example, the Fedora 12 distribution is usually located in a directory fedora/linux/releases/12/that contains separate subdirectories for all supported architectures. CD / DVD image files are stored in a directory iso/. Therefore, you can find the Fedora 12 DVD image for x86_64 computers in the directory fedora/linux/releases/12/Fedora/x86_64/iso/Fedora-12-x86_64-DVD.iso.

Bittorrent

BitTorrent allows you to download files when interacting with other computers. Each computer in the group receives information in parts from the distributing computers. If the data download is completed, the computer goes to the distribution side , that is, it provides this data to other computers for download.

If your computer doesn't have software installed for BitTorrent, visit the BitTorrent home page at http://www.bittorrent.com/download/ to download it. BitTorrent client software is available for Windows, Mac OS, Linux, and many other operating systems.

Mirror for BitTorrent files. Participates in a nearby group. To download and use the Fedora BitTorrent files, visit http://torrent.fedoraproject.org/ .

Minimum boot images

Minimum bootable CD and USB images are not available on the BitTorrent network.

How to find out the architecture of my computer?

Releases are separated by architecture, or type of computer processor. Your computer is according to the type of processor. Consult your manufacturer's documentation for details on your processor, if necessary.

The manufacturer of the processor and its model	Type of architecture for Fedora
Intel (except Atom 230, Atom 330, Core 2 Duo, Centrino Core2 Duo, vintage Xeon); AMD (with the exception of Athlon 64, Athlon x2, Sempron 64, Opteron); VIA C3, C7	i386
Intel Atom 230, Atom 330, Core 2 Duo, Centrino Core 2 Duo, Xeon; AMD Athlon 64, Athlon x2, Sempron64, Opteron; Apple MacBook, MacBook Pro, MacBook Air	x86_64
Apple Macintosh G3, G4, G5, PowerBook and other non-intel models	ppc

i386 Suitable for most Windows compatible computers

If you do not know the processor model, select i386.

The computer is a non-Intel based Apple Macintosh. Refer to Table, "Processor Types and Architectures" for more information.

Intel Atom architectures may vary.

The N and Z Series Atom processors are based on the i386 architecture. The 230 and 330 Series Atom processors are based on the x86_64architecture. Refer to http://ark.intel.com/cpugroup.aspx?familyID=29035 for more details.

What files need to be downloaded?

Below are ways to boot Fedora.

Each file type includes the following: For example, the DVD file distribution of the Fedora 12 for x86_64 is named Fedora-12-x86_64-DVD.iso. "How to find out the architecture of my computer?" If you are unsure of your computer's architecture.

Full distribution on DVD

If you have a fast Internet connection, free time and the desire to get maximum freedom in choosing programs, download the full DVD version. Create a bootable disc by burning the resulting image onto a DVD. In case of problems, this disk can also serve as a recovery. The full version can be downloaded from the mirror server or via BitTorrent.

Live image

Install it on your computer. If your computer supports booting from a CD or USB, you can boot it up. After downloading the image to the hard drive. Just click on it to install Fedora on your hard drive. Live images can be downloaded from a mirror server or via BitTorrent.

Minimum bootable media

If you have a fast Internet connection, but you don't want to download the entire distribution, you can download a bootable CD image for a minimal Fedora environment that allows you to perform a network installation. And although this method involves downloading a fairly large amount of information, it will still not exceed the size of the full distribution. If desired, programs can be added or removed after installation.

Download size

Installing a standard set of Fedora packages over the Internet takes longer than a Live image, but less than a distribution on a DVD. Of course, the impact will be on both the network traffic and the software you chose to install.

Files on the mirror server. Instead, architectures spec the architecture of the computer.

Media type	File location
Full distribution on DVD	fedora/linux/releases/12/Fedora/arch/iso/Fedora-12-arch-DVD.iso
Live image	fedora/linux/releases/12/Live/архитектура/iso/Fedora-12-архитектура-Live.iso, fedora/linux/releases/12/Live/архитектура/iso/Fedora-12-KDE-архитектура-Live.iso
Minimum bootable CD	fedora/linux/releases/12/Fedora/arch/os/images/boot.iso

Table 2.2. File location

How can I create Fedora installation media?

The ISO file can be burned to a CD or DVD. You can also save Live image files to a CD, DVD, or USB device.

Creating CD / DVDs

To learn how to turn ISO images into CD or DVD media, refer to http://docs.fedoraproject.org/readme-burning-isos/ .

Create USB media

You can create bootable USB media in a Windows or Linux system using a Fedora Live image.

When creating a USB-image data is saved

When you write a Live image to a USB drive, the existing data on it will remain intact.

217

It is always a good idea to complete sensitive disk operations.

First make sure the USB device has enough free space. There is no need to re-format or partition it. It is recommended that you back up important data before performing critical operations.

Creating a USB Image in Windows

Download the LiveUSB Creator program for Windows from http://fedorahosted.org/liveusb-creator.

Creator LiveUSB CAN the create the live an either the USB media from an image file That you downloaded the Previously, as with the Described in Section 2.1.3, "Which Files Do I Download?» , Or IT CAN download an image file from the of Internet. Either:

Click the Browse button under the text Use an existing LiveCD and select a preloaded ISO image.

In the LiveUSB creation program window, select the Fedora Live ISO image from the drop-down menu below the Download Fedora text. Please note that the image size is quite large, so you should not download the file in the absence of broadband Internet access.

Click Create Live USB.

Creating a USB Image on Linux

USB drives are most often flash drives or a connected external drive. Usually on such devices the vfat file system is created. In general, they can be formatted as ext2, ext3, vfat.

Btrfs

The GRUB loader does not support the btrfs file system. Therefore, you cannot use bootable USB media with btrfs.

Non-standard USB media

Sometimes, if there are USB-carriers with non-standard formatting and partitioning scheme, the image recording can fail.

Depending on the Linux distribution you are using, choose one of the following methods to create LiveUSB:

Creating LiveUSB on Fedora, Red Hat Enterprise Linux and similar Linux distributions

You can use graphical or text utilities to create LiveUSB in Fedora and Red Hat Enterprise Linux.

Red Hat Enterprise Linux and Similar Systems

It is possible to enable the Extra Packages for Enterprise Linux (EPEL) repository. Refer to

http://fedoraproject.org/wiki/EPEL/FAQ#howtouse

for instructions.

Creating LiveUSB in Graphic Mode

Install the liveusb-creator package using the graphical package manager or execute the installation command:

su -c 'yum -y install liveusb-creator'

Connect the USB drive.

Launch the LiveUSB creation program. To do this, either select it from the menu, or simply execute the command liveusb-creator. When prompted, enter the root password.

Creator LiveUSB CAN the create the live an either the USB media from an image file That you downloaded the Previously, "Which Files Do I Download? Or IT CAN download an image file from the Internet. Either:

Click the Browse button under the text Use an existing LiveCD and select a preloaded ISO image.

In the LiveUSB creation program window, select the Fedora Live ISO image from the drop-down menu below the Download Fedora text. Please note that the image size is quite large, so you should not download the file in the absence of broadband Internet access.

Click Create Live USB.

Create LiveUSB in text mode

The Install the livecd-tools package on your system with your graphical package manager Have, or the following command:

su -c 'yum -y install livecd-tools'

Connect the USB drive.

Determine the device name for the USB media. If the media name is a volume name, then the device name can be found in /dev/disk/by-labelor execute the command

su -c 'findfs LABEL = " MyLabel"'

If you are unsure or the media name is not a volume name, refer to the log /var/log/messages:

su -c 'less / var / log / messages'

To write the image to the media, use the command livecd-iso-to-disk:

su -c 'livecd-iso-to-disk the_image.iso/ dev / sdX1'

Replace sdX1the device name with USB media. Most flash drives and external hard drives use just one partition. If for some reason you have changed it or used a non-standard partition scheme, you will need to further study how to work with it.

Creating LiveUSB in other Linux distributions

To create LiveUSB Fedora on a computer running Linux, but not Fedora or Red Hat Enterprise Linux, you can use either a graphical distribution application or a text-based workflow already described.

This is a graphical tool that allows you to create live Linux distributions. The Fedora Project does not distribute UNetbootin - it is available from http://unetbootin.sourceforge.net/ . This is where you can find out how to use it.

The sequence of actions for creating LiveUSB Fedora on the command line:

Download a live ISO file for Fedora as shown in Section 2.1.3, "Which files do I need to download?"

Connect the USB drive.

Determine the device name for the USB media. If the media name is a volume name, then the device name can be found in /dev/disk/by-labelor execute the command

su -c 'findfs LABEL = " MyLabel"'

If you are unsure or the media name is not a volume name, refer to the log /var/log/messages:

su -c 'less / var / log / messages'

Usually, Linux distributions automatically mount USB devices when they are connected. In this case, disconnect the device. The actions may differ for different distributions. The overall sequence is:

select File> Unmount if it displays the contents of the device.

Open the context menu by right-clicking on the device icon and select Disable.

Click on the icon that allows you to remove the drive - usually looks like a triangle.

At the command prompt, follow su -to enter root mode, enter the root password.

Create a mount point for the downloaded Live image. For example, run the command mkdir /tmp/livecdto mount an image to a point /tmp/livecd.

Mount the Live image: where is the location of the image file, is the file itself, and the created connection point. mount -o loop / path / to the file / image / file.iso / path / to the point / path / to the file / image / file.iso/ way / to the pointGo to the mounted directory. For example, to go to the LiveOSrun command cd /tmp/livecd/LiveOS.

This is a USB device. ./livecd-iso-to-disk / path / to / file / image / file.iso device / path / to / file / image / file.iso device

The image is Fedora-12-i686-Live.isouploaded to a directory Downloadsin the home directory. Flash drive connected to computer as /dev/sdc1.

Switch to root mode:

su -

Create a point to mount the image:

mkdir / mnt / livecd

Connect image:

mount -o loop / home / пользователь/Downloads/Fedora-12-i686-Live.iso / mnt / livecd

Go to the LiveOSimage directory :

cd / mnt / livecd / liveOS

Run the livecd-iso-to-disk command to transfer the image to a flash drive and make it bootable:

./livecd-iso-to-disk / home / пользователь/Downloads/Fedora-12-i686-Live.iso / dev / sdc1

Example 2.1. Mounting the Fedora Live image and creating LiveUSB using the livecd-isc-to-disk

Getting Fedora on CD / DVD

There is no problem with the download of the media. There is a minimal cost. Use your favorite web search engine to locate a vendor, or refer to http://fedoraproject.org/wiki/Distribution.

Part I. Before you begin

This part of the Fedora Installation Guide lists issues that should be considered before proceeding with the installation of Fedora. These include:

Deciding whether to install a new copy of Fedora or upgrade an existing installation.

Information about the equipment and its capabilities that should be considered for installation.

preparing for the Fedora network installation.

Is your hardware compatible?

Compatibility of equipment is of great importance if you have a rather old system or you have built it yourself. Fedora 12 is compatible with most hardware in systems released over the past two years. However, equipment specifications change almost daily, so it is difficult to ensure that your equipment is 100% compatible.

An updated list of supported hardware can be found in the Fedora 12 release notes at http://docs.fedoraproject.org/release-notes .

You must be able to complete your computer hardware configuration (refer to Section 14.4, "Hardware Profile"). You can view the statistics gathered by http://smolt.fedoraproject.org/static/stats/devices.html. It can help you determine how much your hardware is.

You can also refer to the hardware compatibility list on LinuxQuestions.org:

http://www.linuxquestions.org/hcl/index.php

Is there enough disk space?

Nearly every modern-day operating system (OS) uses disk partitions, and Fedora is no exception. When you install Fedora, you may have to work with disk partitions. If you haven't had a quick review of the basic concepts, refer to Appendix A, Introduction to disk partitions before proceeding.

The disk space used in Fedora must be separated from the space occupied by other operating systems installed on your system, such as Windows, OS / 2, or even another version of Linux. The platform x86, AMD64 and Intel ® 64 Fedora system should be allocated at least two partitions (/and swap).

Before installation is necessary

provide enough unallocated [1] disk space to install Fedora or

make sure that the system has one or more partitions that can be deleted and, thus, free up disk space for installing Fedora.

To gain a better sense of how much space you really need, refer to the recommended partitioning sizes, "Recommended Partitioning Scheme" .

If you are not ready to use the installation, refer to Appendix A, Understanding Disk Partitions.

Is it possible to install from a CD / DVD?

You can install Fedora in a variety of ways.

To install from a CD / DVD, you will need a Fedora 12 CD or DVD and a CD / DVD drive on a system that can boot from CD / DVD.

Boot from your DVD / CD-ROM drive. For more information about changing your BIOS, "Booting the Installation Program on x86, AMD64 and the Intel ® 64" .

Alternative boot methods

Bootable CD / DVD

If you can boot using the DVD / CD-ROM drive, you can create your own CD-ROM drive to boot the installation program. This may be useful for example, if you are on a hard drive, "Creating a bootable installation CD" for further instructions.

USB pen drive

If you cannot boot from a CD / DVD, you can also boot from a USB device, for example, from a USB flash drive.

This boot option requires that the BIOS supports booting from a USB device.

The the Install the livecd-tools package on your system with your graphical package manager Have, or the the following command:

su -c 'yum -y install livecd-tools'

The download boot.isoimage file, "Which Files Do I Download?» And the use the livecd-the iso-to-disk script to copy-IT to your the USB device:

livecd-iso-to-disk /path/k/file/image/boot.iso device

Here / path / to the file / image / boot.isois the USB boot device. Example:

livecd-iso-to-disk '/home/username/Downloads/boot.iso' / dev / sdc1

You use of Red the if Hat Enterprise the Linux or a the Linux distribution derived View from IT, you CAN Obtain the the livecd-tools package from the Extra the Packages for the Linux Enterprise (EPEL) repository. Refer to

http://fedoraproject.org/wiki/EPEL/FAQ#howtouse   for
details.

To create bootable USB media from a file boot.isoon
Microsoft Windows or Linux systems not based on Red Hat
Enterprise Linux or Fedora, you will need to find utilities
that are suitable for a specific operating system.

This is a graphical tool that can be used to create a live
Windows Linux distribution. The Fedora Project does not
distribute   UNetbootin   -   it   is   available   from
http://unetbootin.sourceforge.net/ . This is where you can
find out how to use it.

Creating a bootable installation CD

Of The boot.isoimage file is available for download from
the Same | That servers host the images of the Fedora
installation disks, "Booting the Fedora. You can burn the CD
and the CD program. If you are using a CD-ROM drive, you
must be able to boot from this CD-ROM drive.

Choose a CD based image burn

When you burn the boot.isoimage, make sure you select
the burn an image file to discCD burning software. The
word "image" should be included. Note that not all CD
burning software includes this option. In particular, the CD

burning software built into Microsoft Windows XP and Windows Vista does not offer this capability. There are many programs available that add this capability to Windows operating systems; Infrarecorder is a free and open-source example available from http://www.infrarecorder.org/ .

Preparing for network installation

Note

Make sure you have a CD / DVD drive. Having a CD in the drive may cause unexpected errors.

Ensure that you have a USB storage device such as a flash drive.

The installation data for Fedora must be available when performing network (via NFS, FTP or HTTP) and local installations. Follow the steps below to perform a network installation.

An NFS, FTP, or HTTP server used when performing a network installation must be a separate, dedicated computer that can provide access to the entire contents of the installation DVD (or a set of CDs).

Note

The Fedora installation program has the ability to verify the integrity of installation media. This is relevant for CD, DVD, hard disk images, as well as ISO installation methods available via NFS. It is recommended to check all installation media before starting the installation and do not rush to report errors (most of the errors are in fact due to incorrectly recorded CDs). To validate, type in the invitationboot:

linux mediacheck

Note

Find the name of the directory / location / on / disk /, which is located on the server. The view / export / directory is a directory accessible via FTP, NFS or HTTP. For example, the form / position / on / disk / may contain / var / isos, but / export / directory / directory / http / html / f12 .

In order to copy files from the installation DVD (or a set of CDs) to a Linux computer that will act as an installation server, follow these steps:

Create an ISO image with the command:

dd if=/dev/dvd of=/location/of/disk/space/f12.iso

where dvdis the DVD device.

Instructions for preparing for a network installation using a CD-ROM can be found in the file README-enin disk1.

Preparing for FTP and HTTP installation

Get the files from the ISO image of the installation DVD / CD and put them in a directory that can be accessed by FTP or HTTP access.

Make sure the directory is accessible via FTP or HTTP. Try to connect to it from the server and any other machine belonging to the same network where you are going to perform the installation.

Preparing to install on NFS

For an NFS installation, it is not necessary to mount an ISO image. Enough to provide access to the image over the network. To do this, move all the ISO images to the exported catalog:

for DVD:

mv   /location/of/disk/space/f12.iso
/publicly/available/directory/

for CD-ROM:

mv   /location/of/disk/space/f12-disk*.iso
/publicly/available/directory/

where / public / directory / is the directory specified / etc / exportsfor NFS export.

To export to a specific system:

/publicly/available/directory client.ip.address

To export to all systems, the entry should look like this:

/publicly/available/directory *

Start the NFS daemon (run on Fedora /sbin/service nfs start). If NFS is already running, reload the configuration file (/sbin/service nfs reload).

Preparing to install from hard disk

Note

Installing from a hard disk is only possible with ext2, ext3, or FAT file systems. If the file system is different from those listed, installation from the hard disk will be impossible.

Installing from a hard disk requires the use of ISO images. An ISO image is a file containing an exact copy of a DVD / CD-ROM image. By placing the required Fedora images in a directory, you can install from the hard disk by specifying this directory to the installer.

Ensure that you have a USB storage device such as a flash drive.

To prepare the system for installation from a hard disk, you must configure it in one of the following ways:

Using a set of CD / DVDs - create an ISO image for each installation CD. Run the following command on a Linux system for each disk:

dd if=/dev/cdrom of=/tmp/file-name.iso

Using ISO images - transfer them to the computer where the system will be installed.

Image files must be located either on a local hard drive or on a drive connected via USB. Additionally, you need to copy the file install.imgfrom the image to the directory images- this file is used to install Fedora on computers without CD / DVD drives and without a network connection.

Making sure that you have the correct ISO images before starting the installation, you can avoid problems that often arise when installing from a hard disk. To check the ISO images, use the md5sum program (various md5sum implementations exist on different operating systems). The md5sum program should be located on the same server as the ISO images.

Note

The Fedora installation program has the ability to verify the integrity of installation media. This is relevant for CD, DVD, hard disk images, as well as ISO installation methods available via NFS. It is recommended to check all installation media before starting the installation and do not rush to report errors (most of the errors are in fact due to incorrectly recorded CDs). To validate, type in the invitationboot:

linux mediacheck

In addition, if there is a file in the installation directory updates.img, it will be used for the update anaconda. For more information on how to install Fedora and update the installer, refer to the install-methods.txtRPM package file anaconda.

The sequence of actions for obtaining a file install.imgfrom the image:

```
mount -t iso9660 /path/to/Fedora12.iso /mnt/point -o
loop,ro

cp -pr /mnt/point/images /path/images/

umount /mnt/point
```

Before you begin the installation, check the partition type to ensure that Fedora can read it. To check for a partition's file system under Windows, use the Disk Management tool. To check for a partition's file system under Linux, use the fdiskutility.

Installation from LVM partitions is not possible.

It is not allowed to use ISO files in LVM-managed sections.

[1] Unallocated disk space is free space not occupied by any data sections. When partitioning a disk, each section functions as a separate disk.

System Specification

The installation of your computer's hardware. Although it is necessary to install Fedora "Is Your Hardware Compatible?")

However, some details may be important and even necessary when performing certain types of installations.

So, if you plan to create your own partition structure, write the following:

The model numbers of the connected hard drives, their size, type, and interfaces. Example: Seagate ST3320613AS 320 GB for SATA0, Western Digital WD7500AAKS 750 GB for SATA1. Knowing this data will help identify hard drives during the partitioning process.

If you are installing Fedora as an additional operating system over the existing one, write the following:

Connection points of existing sections. Example: /booton sda1, /on sda2, /homeon sdb1. This will help identify partitions during the partitioning process.

When installing from an image on a local hard drive, note the following:

The hard drive and directory that holds the image, "Location of ISO images for different partition types for the examples.

When installing from a network or iSCSI target, note the following:

Manufacturer and model number of network adapters. Example: Netgear GA311. This will allow adapters to be identified during manual network configuration.

IP, DHCP and BOOTP addresses

Net mask

Gateway ip address

One or more name server (DNS) IP addresses

If any of these network settings are unknown to you, contact your network administrator for assistance.

When installing from a network, note the following:

FTP server, HTTP (web) server, or NFS "Installing from NFS" for examples.

If you plan to install on an iSCSI target, note the following:

The location of the iSCSI target. CHAP username and password -, "Advanced Storage Options" .

If the computer is part of a domain:

Make sure that the domain name is provided by the DHCP server, otherwise you will need to enter the domain name during the installation process manually.

Part II. Installation process

The following sections describe the installation process, starting from choosing the installer boot method and ending with the final system restart. This part of the manual also includes a part on troubleshooting the installation process.

The following procedure will allow you to run the installer from bootable media, Live image, or DVD.

Power off the computer.

Disconnect any external FireWire or USB disks, "FireWire and USB" for more information.

Insert the installation media and turn on the computer.

To boot from installation media, you may need to press a special key or key combination. Most computers will show a message shortly after power up, asking to press a given key to select a boot device. More information about this can be found in the documentation of the computer or motherboard. On Apple computers, pressing the C key will boot the system from the DVD, and earlier versions of Apple hardware may require you to press the Cmd + Opt + Shift + Del combination.

Your computer does the if not the allow you to not boot the select a device as with the IT STARTS up closeup, Up

Need you of might to the configure your system's Basic the Input / the Output the System (the BIOS) to not boot from the media.

To change your BIOS settings on an x86, on AMD64 machines, the Intel ® 64 system, watch the text on the screen when the computer boots. As soon as you see a message about which key you need to press to go to the BIOS, click it.

In the BIOS window that opens, find the section for changing the boot order. The default boot order is C, A, or A, C (from hard disk [C] or floppy disk [A]). Change the order so that the CD-ROM is at the top of the list. Then, the presence of a bootable CD in the drive will be checked first and, if it is not found, only then will it be transferred to the hard disk or diskette.

Save the changes before exiting the BIOS. For further information, refer to the accompanying documentation of your computer.

Interrupt installation

To interrupt the installation process, press Ctrl + Alt + Del or turn off the power to the computer. You can safely cancel the installation before writing changes to partitions on the disk. After that, as a result of the installation interruption, the computer will remain inoperative.

Boot menu

First, a graphical boot menu appears, prompting you to select one of the options. If no selection is made within 60 seconds, the standard boot option will be selected. To select the standard option, you can simply press Enter, and to make another choice, go to the desired line using the arrows and press Enter. You can also customize the boot options; To do this, press Tab.

Boot options

For a listing and explanation of common boot options, refer to Chapter 8, Boot Options.

When booting from live media, press any key to open the boot options menu. Available options:

Download

Used by default. In this case, only startup programs and the kernel will be loaded into memory. This option is recommended for systems with a small amount of memory, since programs will be loaded from disk as they are used.

Check and download

This is a live CD environment, "Media Verification" for more information on the verification process.

Memory check

This option runs an exhaustive test. For more information, "Loading Memory Test Mode (RAM) . "

Download from local disk

Allows you to boot the system from the first installed disk. If the media was loaded ɔy mistake, use this option tɔ immediately boot the system from the hard disk without running the installer.

When booting from a DVD, a restoring CD or from a minimum load media, the following boot options will bɘ available:

Install or update an existing system

The standard choice used by default. Installs Fedora in graphical mode.

Install a system with a standard video driver

Allows you to install Fedora in graphical mode, even if the installation program failed to load the video driver. If the image on the screen disapɔears or is distorted when you select Install or upgrade an existing system, restart the computer and try using this option.

Restore installed system

This option will fix the problem that does not allow booting normally. The Fedora platform is exceptionally stable, but in rare cases loading difficulties are likely. The recovery environment includes special programs that allow you to fix most known problems.

Download from local disk

(for livecd)

Memory check

(for livecd)

Install from another source

When you run all bootable media with the exception of the DVD distribution, the installation source selection menu (hard disk, network share, etc.) will be shown. If you do not want to install the system from a DVD, but boot from a DVD, press Tab in the menu that opens. At the end of the line, add a space and enter linux askmethod.

Fedora can be installed from disk-based images or over a network using NFS, FTP or HTTP. Experienced users quite often resort to these methods of installation, since the speed of reading data from a hard disk or from a network resource is much faster than the speed of a CD or DVD.

The table below lists the different boot methods and recommended installation methods.

Loading method	Installation method
DVD	DVD, network or hard drive
Minimum Boot CD, USB or Recovery Disk	Network or hard drive
Live CD or USB	the application installed on the hard disk

Ways to download and install

"Choosing an Installation Method" contains detailed information about installing from alternate locations.

Media Check

Available installation DVD and LiveCD media allow you to perform integrity checks. When creating discs at home, recording errors are not excluded, which can interrupt the started installation process. To avoid this, it is recommended to check the integrity of the media.

Check Live CD

When booting from the LiveCD, in the boot menu, select Check & Download. The scan will start automatically and if it completes successfully, the LiveCD will continue downloading. Otherwise, you will have to create a new LiveCD from the downloaded image.

DVD check

When booting from the Fedora DVD, you are prompted to check the media after selecting the installation. If successful, the installation process will continue. Otherwise, you will have to create a new DVD from the downloaded image.

Network boot with PXE

To boot with PXE, you need to configure your computer that supports PXE. PXE server, refer to Chapter 10, Setting up the installation server.

Configure network boot for your system. This can be done in the BIOS, usually these options can be labeled as Network Bootor Boot Services. After that, the computer will be ready to boot Fedora without using local media.

To boot a computer from a PXE server:

- Make sure the network cable is connected. The light indicator for connecting a network socket should be lit even if the computer is turned off.
- Turn on the computer.
- A menu will appear. Click the number corresponding to your choice.

Diagnosing PXE Problems

If the computer does not boot from the server, make sure that the network interface is selected as the boot device in the BIOS settings. It is worth noting that some BIOSes do not support the PXE standard. Exact information can be found in the documentation of your computer.

PXE installation with multiple network interfaces

Some servers with multiple network interfaces may not assign the name "eth0" to the first interface. This may result in the installer trying to use a different interface, and not one that is already used by PXE. To change this, pxelinux.cfg/*add the following to the configuration file:

IPAPPEND 2

APPEND ksdevice=bootif

These options will force the installer to use the network interface that is already used by the BIOS and PXE. You can also define the following parameter:

ksdevice=link

In doing so, the installer will use the first detected network device that is connected to the network switch.

Graphic and text interface

Fedora 12 supports text and graphics installation. In this case, the installer image must be placed in RAM or located on a local device (installation DVD or Live media). Therefore, only systems with more than 192 MB of RAM or systems booting from live installation media or DVDs can use the graphics mode. Systems with less than 192 MB of RAM will automatically use text mode. If you prefer text mode anyway, boot:run the command at the prompt linux text.

The transition to text mode will also occur in the following cases:

The system could not identify the monitor hardware.

The system has less than 192 megabytes of RAM.

You have chosen text mode in the boot menu.

The text setup has the same functions as the graphical one, with the exception of partitioning, which is greatly simplified in text mode, and the bootloader configuration and package selection are done automatically. All this can be changed using the GUI after the installation is completed.

Using graphics mode

In text mode Installing does not prevent you from using a graphical interface on your system once it is installed. If you have trouble, it can help as discussed in "Getting Help."

At least 64 MB of RAM required for installation

The installation cannot be continued if the system does not have enough RAM (at least 64 MB).

Installation on platforms, the Intel ® and AMD

This section describes installing Fedora from a DVD / CD-ROM using a graphical, mouse-oriented installer. The following topics will be covered:

- Familiar with the installation program
- Running the installer
- Choosing an installation method
- Settings made during installation (language selection, keyboard, mouse, disk partitioning, etc.)
- Installation completion

GUI installer

If you used a graphical user interface (GUI) earlier, then you are undoubtedly already familiar with the order of work -

how to move the mouse pointer around the screen, press buttons, fill in text input fields.

You can also navigate between interface elements using the keyboard. The Tab key allows you to move around the screen between the input fields, Up and Down scroll through the lists, + and - expand and collapse the lists, Space and Enter executes or deselects the selected item. It is also possible to use the Alt + key combination Xas an alternative method of pressing the buttons or making a selection on the screen (Xreplaced by any on-screen character highlighted with an underscore)

Note

If you are using an x86, AMD64, or the Intel ® 64 and do not want to use the GUI installation program, you can perform the installation in text mode. To run the installer in text mode, run the boot:following command at the prompt :

linux text

"The Boot Menu" for a description of the Fedora boot menu, "Text Interface Setup Program" for a brief description of the installation program.

It is strongly recommended to perform the installation in graphical mode. The graphical installer provides the full functionality of the Fedora installer, including an LVM setting that is not available when installed in text mode.

Users who will still perform the installation in text mode can follow the instructions for installing in graphical mode to get all the necessary information.

Screenshots of the installation process

Anaconda allows you to take screenshots during the installation process. To do this, simply press the key combination Shift + Print Screen and anaconda will save the snapshot to/root/anaconda-screenshots.

If you are performing a kickstart installation, use it autostep --autoscreenshotautomatically, "Creating a Kickstart File" for details of configuring a Kickstart file.

Virtual consoles

The Fedora installation program is more than just a set of installation dialog boxes. You will also encounter various types of diagnostic messages, and you can also enter commands at the shell prompt. The installer displays these messages on five virtual consoles, which you can switch between using a simple key combination.

A virtual console is a command line text shell available locally on a computer. Possible simultaneous access to multiple virtual consoles.

Can be helpful if you encounter a problem while installing Fedora. You can pinpoint a problem. "Consoles, Keyboard Shortcuts , and Their Purposes".

There is usually no need to switch from the default console (virtual console # 6 for installation in graphical mode) unless you are trying to analyze installation problems.

console	keyboard shortcuts	content
one	ctrl + alt + f1	setup dialog
2	ctrl + alt + f2	shell prompt
3	ctrl + alt + f3	installation log (installer messages)
four	ctrl + alt + f4	system messages
five	ctrl + alt + f5	other messages
6	ctrl + alt + f6	graphic display

Consoles, keyboard shortcuts and their purpose

Setup text interface

Comment

Installation for Fedora. If you are installing a VNC connection, Installation via VNC .

Your system has the if a graphical display, But graphical installation fails, the try not booting with the xdriver=vesaoption - see Chapter 8, Boot Options

252

The Fedora text mode of The installation program uses clause a screen-based interface includes That will most of the on-screen widgets commonly found! On graphical user interfaces, "Installation Program Widgets Configuration " , "Installation Program Widgets Configuration " , illustrate screens during the installation process.

The cursor is used to select and act on a specific item. When you move the cursor from one element to another, the elements may change color, and in some cases the cursor will be located inside or near the element.

Note

It is not explicitly documented. However, it is not necessary to provide an example of a stream of insatallation process, which is also available in text mode. This guide notes:

Customizing the partition layout.

Customizing the bootloader configuration.

Selecting packages during installation.

Note also that it is possible to manipulate the logical volume management. In text mode it is possible to view and accept the default LVM setup.

Note

Not all languages supported by textual installation are supported in graphical mode. This especially applies to groups of languages that do not use Latin or Cyrillic. If you choose a language that is not supported in text mode, the installation process will use English.

Legend

Window - Windows (often referred to as dialogs in this manual) will appear on the screen during installation. Sometimes one window can overlap another, in such cases you can work only in the top window. When you finish working with it, it will disappear, making the window below available.

Checkbox - allows you to select an item or deselect it. The status of the checkbox is indicated by an asterisk '*' (selected) or a space (not selected). Having placed the cursor on the checkbox, press Space to set or reset it.

Text entry field - Areas for entering information required for installation. When the cursor is located in the text entry field, you can enter and / or edit information in this field.

Legend

Text blocks - Areas of the screen in which text is displayed. Sometimes controls can contain other controls, such as checkboxes. If the text block contains more information than can be displayed in the specified area, a scroll bar appears; If you position the cursor in a text box, you can use the Up and Down keys to view its contents. The current position will be marked in the scroll bar with a # symbol that will move up and down when scrolling.

Scroll Bar - Scroll down to the bottom of the window frame. Scroll bar

Button - buttons are the main method of interaction with the installer. The transition between windows is carried out using buttons, as well as Tab and Enter keys. Buttons can be pressed, and then they are displayed highlighted.

Using the keyboard to navigate

Moving between dialogs is done with a few keys. Use the left, right, up and down arrow keys to move the cursor. Use the Tab and Alt - Tab keys to move from one screen element to another. At the bottom of the screen, the keyboard shortcuts used to move the cursor are usually shown.

"Press" the button (using Tab, for example) and press Space or Enter. The select an item the To from a list of items, the move the cursor to the item you wish to the select and press the Enter. The select an item the To with a checkbox Central, the move the cursor to the checkbox Central and press Space to the select an item. To deselect, press Space a second time.

By pressing F12, you agree to the current values and go to the next dialog; this is equivalent to clicking the OK button.

Warning

If you do not need to enter data in the dialog box, do not press any keys during installation (this can lead to unpredictable behavior).

Running the installer

To start, first make sure you have the necessary resources for the installation. If you have already read through in Getting Started, and followed the instructions, you should be ready to start the installation process. If you have verified that you are ready to start, boot the installation program using the Fedora DVD or CD-ROM # 1.

Loading on x86 Setup, AMD64 and the Intel ® 64

The installer can be launched in the following ways (first it is worth checking which boot methods your system supports):

Fedora DVD / CD if the computer supports booting from a DVD / CD and you have a set of Fedora discs.

Boot disk to perform network installation and hard disk installation. In this case, the computer must support booting from CD / DVD.

USB-drive, if the computer supports booting from USB-devices.

PXE boot via network - Your machine supports booting from the network. This is an advanced installation path, Setting up the installation server for additional information on this method.

To create a boot CD-ROM or to prepare your USB drive for installation, "Alternative Boot Methods".

Insert the bootable media and reboot the system.

To boot from installation media, you may need to press a special key or key combination. Most computers will show a message shortly after power up, asking to press a given key to select a boot device. More information about this can be found in the documentation of the computer or motherboard. On Apple computers, pressing the C key will boot the system from the DVD, and earlier versions of Apple hardware may require you to press the Cmd + Opt + Shift + Del combination.

Your computer does the if not the allow you to not boot the select a device as with the IT STARTS up closeup, Up Need you of might to the configure your system's Basic the Input / the Output the System (the BIOS) to not boot from the media.

To change your BIOS settings on an x86, on AMD64 machines, the Intel ® 64 system, watch the text on the screen when the computer boots. As soon as you see a message about which key you need to press to go to the BIOS, click it.

In the BIOS window that opens, find the section for changing the boot order. The default boot order is C, A, or A, C (from hard disk [C] or floppy disk [A]). Change the order so that the CD-ROM is at the top of the list. Then, the presence of a bootable CD in the drive will be checked first and, if it is not found, only then will it be transferred to the hard disk or diskette.

Save the changes before exiting the BIOS. For further information, refer to the accompanying documentation of your computer.

After a short pause, a screen appears with the boot options.

When downloading the installer, note the following:

The installer will start automatically as soon as the prompt appears boot: Press one of the indicated help screen function keys to cancel it.

When you press the help screen function key, you will notice a short delay, which means that at this moment the information is being read from the rescue media, then the help screen will appear.

Normally, you only Up Need to press the Enter to not boot. Be sure to see your hardware. If your hardware is properly detected, continue to the next section. If you are using the boot options, see Boot Options .

Advanced boot options

Although it is easiest to boot from a CD or DVD and perform a graphical installation, sometimes there are situations when you need to boot in another way. This section provides additional options for booting Fedora.

The following instructions are for transmitting parameters x86 loader systems, AMD64, Intel ® 64.

Note

Boot Options for additional boot options not covered in this section.

To perform a text-based installation at the bootloader's prompt, run

linux text

ISO images contain their checksum md5sum. The team checks the integrity of the amount:

linux mediacheck

The installation program will prompt you to insert a CD or select an ISO image for testing and click OK. Checksum checks can be performed for any Fedora CD in random order (you do not need to start the scan from the first disc). It is strongly recommended that you scan all Fedora disks created from downloaded ISO images. This command works when installing from a CD, DVD, ISO image located on your hard disk, and using the network installation method.

Of The boot.isoimage file is available for download from the Same | That servers host the images of the Fedora installation disks - to refer "Booting the Fedora. You can burn the CD and the CD program. If you are using a CD-

ROM drive, you must be able to boot from this CD-ROM drive.

Up Need you to perform the installation in serial mode, the of the type the following command:

linux console=<device>

To start a text installation, run

linux text console=<device>

In the above command, it <device>should be the device you are using (such as ttyS0 or ttyS1). Example for, linux text console=ttyS0.

Text mode installations using a serial terminal work best when the terminal supports UTF-8. Under UNIX and Linux, Kermit supports UTF-8. For Windows, Kermit '95 works well. Non-UTF-8 terminals used during the installation process. An enhanced serial display can be used utf8. For example:

linux console=ttyS0 utf8

Kernel options

You can pass parameters to the kernel. For example, to apply Anaconda installer updates from a floppy disk, type the following:

linux updates

To start a text installation, run

linux text updates

The team will ask you to insert a floppy disk with updates. When performing a network installation and there is an image with updates on the server in the directory rhupdates/, this is not necessary.

After specifying all parameters, press Enter.

If you need to specify them, please write down. The boot options are needed during the boot loader configuration portion of the installation (refer to "Setting the boot loader for x86, AMD64 and the Intel ® 64» for more information).

For more information on kernel options refer to Boot Options.

Choosing an installation method

What installation method will you use? There are the following options:

DVD / CD-ROM

If you have a DVD / CD-ROM drive and the Fedora CD-ROMs or DVD you can use this method. Refer to Section 6.5, "Installing from a DVD / CD-ROM", for DVD / CD-ROM installation instructions.

Hard drive

If you have copied the Fedora ISO, you can use this method. You need a boot CD-ROM (use the linux askmethodor boot option). Refer to "Installing from a Hard Disk" , for hard drive installation instructions. linux repo=hd:device:/path

Nfs

If you are installing from an NFS server using ISO, you can use this method. You need a boot CD-ROM (use the linux askmethodor boot option). Refer to Section 6.8, "Installing with NFS" for network installation instructions. Note that NFS installations may also be in GUI mode. linux repo=nfs:server :options:/path

URL

If you are installing directly from an HTTP (Web) server or FTP server, use this method. You need a boot You CD-ROM (use the linux askmethod, , or boot option). Refer to Section 6.9, "Installing via FTP or HTTP" , for FTP and HTTP installation instructions. linux repo=ftp://user:password@host/pathlinux repo=http://host/path

If you're booted on the DVD, do not use it askmethod. Proceed to Section 6.10, "Welcome to Fedora . "

CD / DVD

When you download any Fedora installation media, the next stage of installation will start from it regardless of the installation method, but the package data will be downloaded from the original source.

Install from DVD / CD-ROM

To install Fedora from a DVD / CD-ROM, insert the first disk and boot from it.

The installer will check the hardware and try to identify the CD-ROM drive by searching for drives with an IDE interface (also called ATAPI devices).

Note

To abort the installation process at this time, reboot your machine and then eject the boot media. CAN the cancel running safely You the installation AT the any point the before the About to the Install screen. Refer to "Installing Packages" for more information.

If the CD-ROM drive is not identified and it has a SCSI interface, then the installation program will prompt you to select the SCSI driver. Select the driver that best fits your adapter. You can specify additional driver options;

however, most drivers will detect the SCSI adapter automatically.

If you are a DVD / CD-ROM drive, you can find it. This wil take some time to skip over this step. However, if you encounter problems with the installer from the media check dialog, continue to the installation process (refer to "Welcome to Fedora").

Install from hard drive

The Select Partition dialog appears if you are installing the system from a disk partition (that is, you selected the Hard Disk in the Installation Method dialog). In this window, you define the name of the disk partition and the directory from which to install Fedora. If you specified a parameter when loading repo=hd, the section can be omitted, since it is already defined.

Select a section with ISO images from the list. The names of internal IDE, SATA, SCSI, USB devices begin with /dev/sd. Each drive has its own letter, for example /dev/sda, a partition on a drive - the number, for example /dev/sda1.

In the Catalog with image field, specify the absolute path. The table below contains some examples:

Partition type	Tom	Source file path	Catalog
VFAT	D: \	D: \ Downloads \ F12	/ Downloads / F12
ext2, ext3, ext4	/ home	/ home / user1 / F12	/ user1 / F12

Layout of ISO images for different types of partitions

If the ISO images are located in the root directory of the partition, enter /. If they are located in the subdirectory of the mounted partition, specify this directory, for example, for images in the directory of the /home/new/connected partition /home/, enter /new/.

Use the "/" symbol

The absence of the "/" symbol at the beginning of the recording may result in a failure of the installation.

Select OK to continue. Proceed with Section 6.10, "Welcome to Fedora . "

Network installation

The installer can interact with network resources. For example, when downloading an installer with a parameter askmethodor repo=you can install Fedora from a network server using FTP, HTTP, NFS protocols. Later in the installation process, you will be able to set up additional repositories.

When performing a network installation, you will see the TCP / IP Setup dialog. This dialog asks for your IP and other network addresses. You can choose to determine the IP address and netmask via DHCP or manually.

The default installer uses DHCP to make network settings. DHCP is fine if you use a cable connection or DSL modem, router, firewall, or other network equipment to communicate with the Internet. If there is no DHCP server, clear the Use dynamic IP configuration (DHCP) check box.

Enter the IP address to be used during the installation and press Enter.

The installation program supports only the IPv4 protocol. Refer also to Section 6.15, "Network Configuration" for more information on configuring your network.

TCP / IP configuration

Upon completion of the installation settings will be applied to the system.

There are many ways to install: on a local or external network, from a web server or NFS server, from a local or public mirror supported by the community. Whenever possible, select the closest server.

The Fedora Project maintains a list of Web and FTP public mirrors, sorted by region, at http://fedoraproject.org/wiki/Mirrors. It is shown on the web page. A correct mirror location for an system resembles the URL. /12/Fedora/architecture/os/i386http://mirror.example.co m/pub/fedora/linux/releases/12/Fedora/i386/os

If you are installing via NFS, proceed to "Installing with NFS".

If you are installing via Web or FTP, proceed to Section 6.9, "Installing via FTP or HTTP" .

Install from NFS

The NFS configuration dialog will appear if you specified a parameter when booting askmethodand selected NFS in the Installation Method window. If you added a parameter repo=nfs, it is assumed that you have already specified the server and path.

Enter the domain name or IP address of your NFS server. For example, if you are installing from a node eastcoastin the domain example.com, enter NFS server nameeastcoast.example.con in the field.

Next, enter the name of the exported directory. If you followed the setup described in Section "Preparing for a Network Installation," you would enter the directory /export/directory/.

If the NFS server is exporting a mirror of the Fedora installation tree, enter the name of the directory containing the base of the installation tree. If everything is correct, a message appears on the screen stating that the Fedora installation program is running.

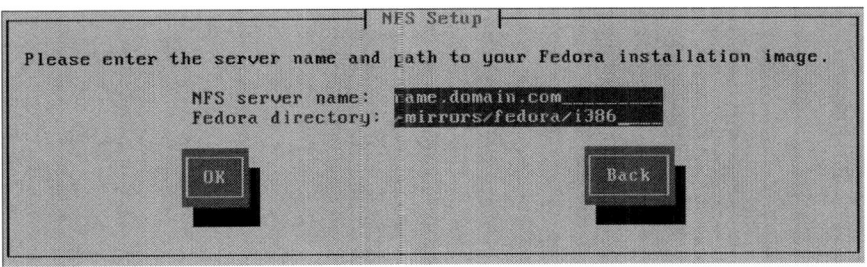

NFS configuration dialog

If the NFS server exports ISO images of Fedora CDs, enter the name of the directory containing these images.

Next, the Welcome dialog appears.

FTP or HTTP installation

When you select a URL in the Installation Method dialog box, a dialog appears that allows you to determine the HTTP or FTP server from which Fedora will be installed.

Enter the link to the installation directory (install.img) on the selected FTP or HTTP site and press Enter. The default will be the directory where it should be replaced with an appropriate value, for example, i386. Then the link might look like this: If everything is configured correctly, a message will appear about the receipt of files from the server.
/pub/fedora/linux/releases/12/Fedora/архитектура/os/images/архитектураhttp://download.fedoraproject.org/pub/fedora/linux/releases/12/Fedora/i386/os/images

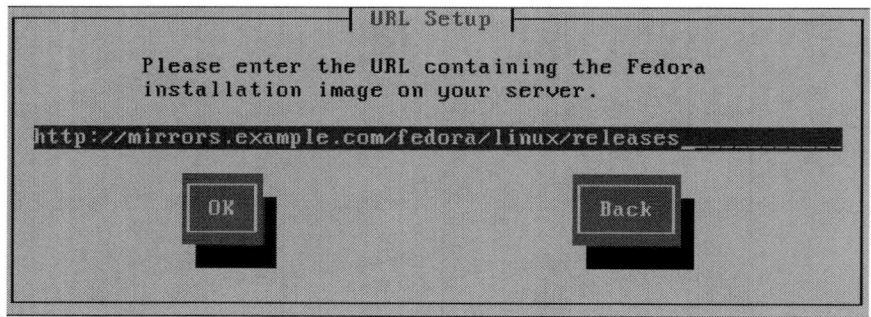

URL setting dialog

Next, the Welcome dialog appears.

Note

You can save disk space by using ISO images that you previously copied to the server. To do this, install Fedora using images without copying them into a separate tree by loopback. For each image run:

mkdir discX

mount -o loop Fedora12-discX.iso discX

Replace Xwith the appropriate disk number.

Welcome to Fedora

The welcome screen does not require any action from you.

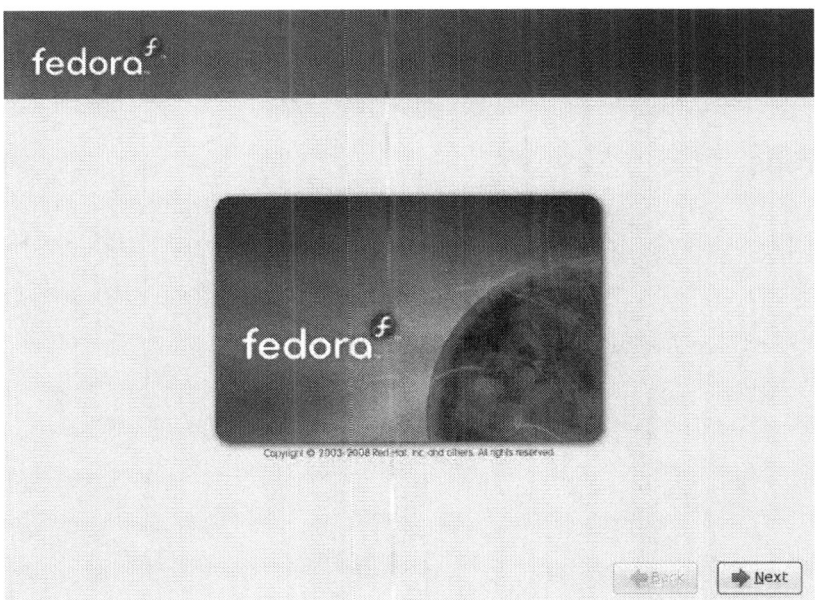

To continue, click Next.

Language selection

Using your mouse to select the language for the installation (refer to "Language Selection").

Selecting the appropriate language also helps determine the time zone settings later in the installation process. The installer attempts to determine the time zone based on the language you specified in this dialog.

To add support for custom languages, customize the installation at the package selection stage. For more information, refer to Section "Support for additional languages. "

Keyboard Configuration

Using the mouse, select the keyboard layout (for example, Russian) that you wish to use for installation and assign it to the system by default (see figure).

After making your selection, click Next to continue.

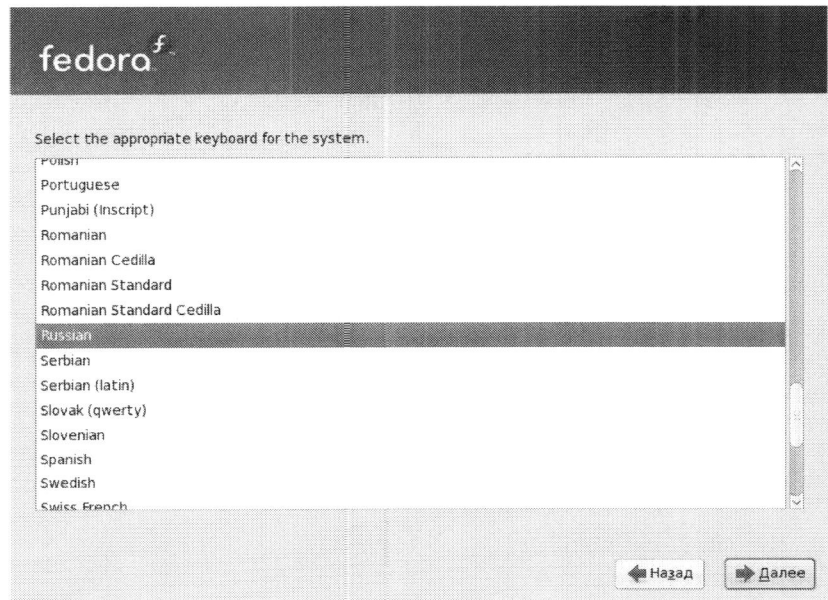

Keyboard Configuration

Fedora includes layout for many languages. Particular with in, will most by European languages include a latin1option, the uses clause dead keys to access certain characters, such as with the diacritical marks. When you press a dead key Example for, to of the type éon a latin1 keyboard layout, you would press (and release) the ' key, and the then press the Ekey. By contrast, you can press and hold down the key (such as Alt-Gr) E. Other keyboards might be a dedicated key for this character.

Note

To change the keyboard layout after installation is complete, use the Keyboard Settings utility.

Run a command at the shell prompt system-config-keyboardto start the keyboard configuration utility. If you are not a root user, you will be prompted to enter the root password to continue.

Hard drive initialization

If no existing partition table is found on the hard disk, the installation program will ask you to initialize the disk. This will make all data on the hard disk become inaccessible for reading. If the system has a new hard disk installed or you have deleted all partitions on the disk, select initialize the disk again.

Warning window - hard disk initialization

It may be the case that some RAID systems and other non-standard configurations of the installation program will not be able to read and will show the request for initializing the hard disk.

Disconnect unnecessary drives.

If you use a non-standard disk configuration, if possible, it is necessary to turn it off during installation: turn off the system, disconnect the disks and restart the installation.

Upgrade existing system

Preupgrade

Fedora provides the preupgrade command-line utility that allows you to upgrade an existing Fedora installation to a new version.

The installation of Fedora. It's not a problem. The hard disk drive doesn't change. Your system configuration changes only if a package upgrade. But it's not a problem.

Note: You need to upgrade your computer. In particular, the Fedora CD is available in Fedora. The update-packages the Two are not included on the installation medium, the make sure the you select the or the repository DURING the package group selection - to refer to Section "Installing from Additional Repositories". Fedora 12 - architectureFedora 12 - architecture - Updates

Select update

If Fedora or Red Hat Linux is already installed on your computer, a dialog box will appear prompting you to upgrade your existing system. To perform an update, you must select the corresponding item from the drop-down list and click Next.

Manually Installed Programs

The behavior of manually installed programs on an existing Fedora or Red Hat Linux system may change. It is possible that they need to be reinstalled.

Upgrade using the installer

Board

In general, the Fedora Project recommends that you /homeperform a fresh installation. For more information on these sections, refer to Section "Disk Partitioning Setup" .

If you choose to upgrade your system, it's not necessary to upgrade your system. Before you start an upgrade

rpm   -qa   --qf   '%{NAME}   %{VERSION}-%{RELEASE} %{ARCH}\n' > ~/old-pkglist.txt

After installation, this list will help determine which packages will need to be reinstalled.

Additionally, back up the system settings:

su -c 'tar czf /tmp/etc-`date +%F`.tar.gz /etc' su -c 'mv /tmp/etc-*.tar.gz /home'

Create backup copies of all important data, such as the contents of a directory /homeand files of Apache servers, FTP, SQL and code management systems. And while updating an existing system does not destroy data, there is a small chance of data loss.

Backup Backup

Note that the examples above save a copy to the directory /home. If the home directory is not located in a separate partition, it is better to save the backup on another device (CD / DVD or external hard disk).

For more information on completing the upgrade process later, refer to Section "Finishing an Upgrade".

Update bootloader configuration

Your completed Fedora installation must be registered in the boot loader to boot properly. A boot loader is the software on your machine that locates and starts the operating system Refer to Section "Configuring boot loader for x86, AMD64 and the Intel ® 64 for more information about not boot of loaders.

The installer will be able to modify the existing standard bootloader so that it downloads the new Fedora system. To do this, select Update bootloader setup. This option will be checked by default when upgrading an existing Fedora system.

GRUB is the standard boot loader for Fedora. The Fedora installer will not be able to update other boot loaders, such as BootMagic™, System Commander™, or the boot loader installed by Microsoft Windows. In this case, select Skip Boot Update. For further help, see your computer's documentation.

If you really want to replace an existing bootloader, please note that after installing a new bootloader it may be that other operating systems will not be able to boot without first setting up a new bootloader. To remove an existing bootloader and install GRUB, select Create a new bootloader configuration.

Click the continue button.

Network configuration

Fedora provides support for IPv4 and IPv6. However, the default installer uses IPv4 for network interfaces and DHCP. Currently NetworkManager does not support IPv6. To configure IPv6 after installation, use system-config-network.

In the format of the node. domain It is possible to specify the network host name.

For most users, the standard choice will be localhost.localdomain.

It is recommended that you set up a network name for your computer. If you have multiple computers, also give them names.

Valid node names

The system can be assigned any unique node name. The name may contain letters, numbers and hyphen characters.

On some networks, the DHCP provider also provides the name of the computer, or hostname. This is a complete hostname, such as machine1.example.com. The machine name (or "short hostname") is machine1, and the domain name is example.com.

If Fedora is directly connected to the Internet, consider the rules of your provider. Their discussion is beyond the scope of this document.

Modem setup

The installation program does not configure modems. Once installed, they can be configured using the network configuration utility. The modem settings will depend on the settings of the ISP.

Manual setting

Settings that require complex configuration will not be able to continue without network access. In cases where the success of the installation depends on the correct network settings, the installation program will open a dialog box where you can confirm them.

If you want to override the interface, select it. Uncheck the box next to Use Dynamic IP Configuration (DHCP). Enter an IPv4 address, a netmask in the format address / mask, a gateway address and a name server.

Click OK to apply the settings.

Time zone setting

Specify the time zone even if you plan to use NTP (Network Time Protocol) to synchronize the clock.

Set your time zone by selecting your city closest to your computer's physical location. Click here to view the map.

Specify the time zone even if you plan to use NTP (Network Time Protocol) to synchronize the clock.

Below are two methods for selecting a time zone:

Click on the map to select a specific city marked with a yellow dot; a red X will indicate your choice.

You can also select a time zone from the list at the bottom of the screen.

If only Fedora is installed on the computer, select System Clock uses UTC . Fedora will then calculate the time difference between local time and UTC. This behavior is standard on UNIX operating systems.

Windows and system clock

Do not select the System Clock option uses UTC if Microsoft Windows is present. The fact is that Microsoft operating systems change BIOS clock settings to match local time and not UTC, which can lead to unpredictable results in Fedora.

Note

To change the time zone settings after the installation is completed, use the date and time setting utility.

Run a command at the shell prompt system-config-dateto start the Date / Time Properties utility. If you are not a root user, you will be prompted to enter the root password to continue.

To run the settings utility Date / Time Properties as a text application, run the command timeconfig.

Click Next to continue.

Set root password

Identifying the root account and password is one of the most important steps in installing the system. The root account is similar to the Administrator account on Microsoft Windows systems. The root account is used to install packages, RPM updates, and basic system maintenance. When logged in as root, the user gets full control over the system.

Note

The root user (also called the superuser) has full access to all system resources; for this reason, logging in as root is recommended only for supporting and administering system operations.

Use the root account only for system administration. Create another account for everyday use. When you need to configure or fix something, run the command su -to switch to root mode. Following these simple rules reduces the likelihood of system damage due to a typo or incorrect command.

Note

To switch to root user mode, in response to a shell prompt, type su -and press Enter. Then enter the root password and press Enter again.

The installation program will prompt you to set a root user password [2] on your system. You cannot proceed to the next stage of the installation program without setting this password.

The root password must be no shorter than 6 characters, while the entered characters are not displayed on the screen. You must enter this password twice; if the passwords do not match, the installation program will ask you to re-enter the password.

You can easily get it. The phone number, character sequence (for example, qwerty), the words password, root, 123456, and anteater are examples of bad passwords. Successful passwords consist of a set of numbers, uppercase and lowercase letters. For example: Aard387vark and 420BMttNT. Remember, the password is case sensitive. If you write a password, keep it in a safe place. However, it is not recommended to record passwords.

Note

Do not use the password examples provided in this manual. Their use is a serious safety hazard.

Note

To change the root password after the installation is complete; you can use the root password setting utility.

Run the command at the shell prompt system-config-rootpasswordto start the root password utility. If you are not a root user, you will be prompted to enter the root password to continue.

Enter the password rootin the root password field. For security reasons, asterisks will be shown instead of characters. Enter the same password in the Confirm field. When finished, click the continue button.

Disk partitioning setup

Partitioning allows you to separate sections. Partitioning is particularly useful if you run multiple operating systems. If you are partitioned, read Appendix A, Understanding Disk Partitions for more information.

In this window, you can choose whether to perform the partition automatically or manually by clicking Create your own partition.

The first four items perform automatic partitioning of the disk into sections without the need to do it manually. If you do not consider yourself an experienced user, it is not recommended to perform manual partitioning, but let the installation program do it for you.

You can configure the orbital recovery configuration button. For more information refer to Section 6.19, Advanced Storage Options.

Warning

PackageKit downloads updated packages by default/var/cache/yum/. If you manually crashed the disks and created a separate partition/var/, check whether there is enough space in this section (at least 3 gigabytes) to download the updated packages.

If you choose to create a custom layout, refer to Section 6.21, "Partitioning a Disk" .

Warning

If at the end of the partitioning configuration stage an error is generated

"It was an unreadable partition. On the drive."

You may not have to be able to use your computer.

Users who have worked with programs such as EZ-BIOS should be familiar with similar problems, leading to final data loss (in case a backup copy of the information was not created before the installation).

If you're not doing so, you should always be made.

RAID and other disk devices

Hardware RAID

A RAID array (Redundant Array of Independent Disks) provides the functionality of a group or array of disks as a whole. Before you begin the installation process, configure all available RAID options. In Fedora, each active RAID array will be represented as a separate disk.

Multiple hard drives on Fedora systems can be combined into a single RAID array, eliminating the need for additional hardware.

286

Software RAID

You can use the Linux software RAID arrays, where RAID functions are controlled by the operating system rather than dedicated hardware. These functions are explained in detail in Section "Disk Partitioning Setup".

FireWire and USB

Some FireWire and USB hard drives may not be recognizec by the Fedora installation mechanism. If the setup of these disks during the installation process is not so important, disconnect them to avoid confusion.

Connection after installation

External FireWire and USB drives can be connected and configured after installation. Basically, they are recognized by the kernel and will immediately be available for use.

Advanced Storage Options

From this screen you can configure an iSCSI (SCSI over TCP / IP) target or FCoE (Fiber channel over ethernet) SAN (storage area network). Refer to Appendix B, iSCSI Drives for an introduction to iSCSI.

Configure iSCSI settings

To configure an ISCSI target, select the ISCSI Parameters' dialog by selecting the Add ISCSI target. Fillin ipsi If the ISCSI target authentication uses CHAP (Challenge Handshake Authentication Protocol) for authentication, enter the CHAP username and password. If your enviroment uses 2-way CHAP (also called "Mutual CHAP"), also enter the reverse CHAP username and password. Click the "Add target" button using this information.

Please note that you can try to connect again with a different IP address of the target device in case of incorrect input. However, to change the name of the initiator iSCSI will have to start the installation from the beginning.

Configure FCoE settings

To configure FCoE SAN, select Add FCoE SAN and click the add disk button.

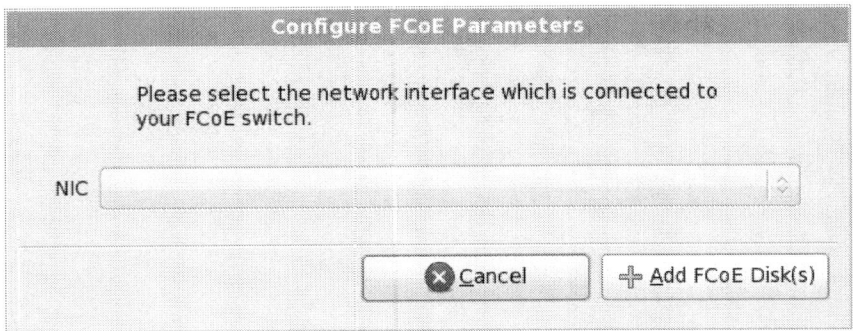

Configure FCoE Parameters

In the next menu, select the interface connected to the FCoE switch and click the add disk button.

Create Default Layout

With automatic disk partitioning, you have the opportunity to determine what data in the system will be affected during the partitioning process. You are offered the following options:

Use entire disk — select this option to delete all partitions on disks (including partitions created by other operating systems, such as Windows VFAT or NTFS partitions).

Warning

If you select this option, the installation program will delete all data from the specified hard drives. Do not select this option if there is data on the hard drive on which you plan to install Fedora, which will still be needed.

Replace existing Linux system - select this option to remove only Linux partitions left from previous Linux installations. However, other sections (for example, VFAT or FAT32) will not be deleted.

Compress an existing system — select this option to reduce the size of existing partitions manually and perform a standard installation of Fedora in the free space.

Warning

Be careful when compressing partitions in which another operating system is installed, as it can be damaged. Although the data from this section will not be deleted, but the operating system requires additional free space. Therefore, before splitting the partition on which another OS is located, make sure that there is still free space.

Use free space - select this option to save existing partitions and their data. It is assumed that there is enough free space on the hard disk.

Create Default Layout

Select the hard drives on which to install Fedora. If there are several hard disks in the system, you can select the disks where the installation will be performed. Unmarked drives and their data will remain intact.

Warning

An excellent idea is to create a backup of all the data on your computer. For example, if you upgrade your system or create a dual boot, you should make a copy of all the data. There is always a chance of errors that can lead to the loss of all data.

Note

If you are using a RAID card, please note that some BIOS options do not support booting from it. In such cases, the partition /boot/should be created outside the RAID array, for example, on a separate disk. If you have problems with RAID controllers, you must use an internal hard disk.

To create software RAIDs, you need a partition /boot/.

If you chose to automatica ly partition your system, you must select the View check box and manually change the partition /boot/.

Select Encrypt system to encrypt all partitions except /boot.

Use the Advanced storage options option if:

If you plan to install Fedora on an iSCSI- connected disk, select Advanced storage options , then Add iSCSI device , select Add disk , specify the IP address and initiator name, and click Add disk .

To disable a dmraid device detected during boot.

To view the selected parameters and make changes to sections created in automatic mode, select the View check box. Then click the continue button to go to the next step, where you will see the sections that anaconda has created. If they do not suit you, you can change these sections as you see fit.

Installing in text mode

When installing in text mode, only the standard partitioning schemes described in this section will be available. In principle, you can choose to use the entire disk or delete existing Linux partitions, but you cannot add or delete partitions or file systems at your own discretion. This requires a kickstart installation or installation in graphical mode via VNC.

Moreover, the advanced features of LVM, resizing and file system encryption are also available only when performing a graphical installation or kickstart.

After making your selection, click Next to continue the installation.

Partitioning a disk

If you chose one of the three automatic partitioning options, didn't select Review, skip ahead to Section "Package Group Selection".

If you decide to perform automatic splitting and choose View, you can accept the suggested default settings (click Next) or change the settings manually.

Comment

Note that when installing in text mode, the modification of logical volumes (LVM) is not possible. You can only view the existing volume structure. Volume configuration can be performed only when performing a graphical installation.

f you chose to create your own partition, at this point you will need to specify where to install Fedora. To do this, you need to define connection points for one or more disk partitions where Fedora will be installed. You may also need to create or delete partitions at this stage.

Note

If you have your partitions, refer to Appendix A, Introduction to Disk Partitions and Section "Recommended Partitioning Scheme." If you're on the system, you're on the system. System users should Itanium have a /boot/efi/partition of approximately 100 MB and of type FAT (VFAT), a swap partition of at least 512 MB, and an appropriately-sized root (/partition).

Except in very rare cases, anaconda can meet the standard disk partitioning requirements.

Graphic representation of hard drives

The partition screen shows a graphical representation of the disk partitioning.

Click in the graphic view to highlight a specific area of the disk. Double-click to edit an existing section or to create a section using free space.

Above the window, the name of the disk (for example, / dev / hda), its size in megabytes and its model (determined by the installation program) will be displayed.

Partitioning screen

These buttons are used to change partition parameters, such as the file system type and mount point, and to create RAID devices. Buttons on the screen are also used to accept the changes made or to close the splitting screen. Next, the buttons are considered in order:

Create: Allows you to add a LVM partition or physical volume. In the Add Partition window, select the mount point and partition type. If there are multiple disks in the system, select the disks on which the partition will be created. Specify the size of the partition in megabytes and optionally select encryption.

Section Restrictions

CAN not the create you is separate partitions for the /bin/, /dev/, /etc/, /lib/, /proc/, /root/, and /sbin/directories. These directories must reside on / (root) partition.

The partition /bootcannot be located in the LVM volume group. Create /bootbefore setting up volume groups. Additionally, you cannot create the btrfs file system in a partition /boot.

Avoid placing /usrin a separate section. If /usrit is not located in the root partition, the boot process becomes much more complicated, which can lead to problems when loading some systems (for example, systems with iSCSI storage will not be able to boot).

Additional options are available for resizing partitions:

Fixed size

Use as close as possible to the specified value size.

Fill all space up to

Increase partition size to specified value.

Fill to maximum allowable size

Increase partition size using all available space on selected disks.

Sizes of sections

In reality, the partition size may slightly differ from the value you specify. This is due to the specifics of the geometry of the disks, and not errors.

To encrypt all the information in the section, select the encryption option.

After you enter your details for your partition, select OK to continue. If you chose to install it, it will help you to assign a passphrase. For hints on using good passphrases, refer to Section "Setting the root Password" .

Edit: Used to change the properties of the partition currently selected in the Sections table. Clicking the Edit buttonbrings up a dialog box. In this window, some or all of the fields can be changed, depending on whether the information about this partition is written to disk or not.

You can also edit the free space shown graphically and create a new section within it. To do this, either allocate free space and click the Edit button, or double-click in this area of the disk.

To create a RAID device, you must first create software RAID partitions (you can also use existing partitions). After creating multiple software RAID partitions, click the RAID button to include these partitions in the RAID array.

Delete: Used to delete the partition currently selected in the Current Partitions area of the disk. Before deleting the section, the program will ask you for confirmation.

To delete an LVM physical volume, first remove the volume groups that include this volume.

If you make a mistake, click Cancel to cancel the changes.

Cancel: Used to return to the original state. All changes will be lost.

RAID: Used to provide redundancy for several or all disk partitions. Use RAID only if you are familiar with this technology.

To create a RAID device, you must first create a software RAID partition. After creating several partitions, click the RAID button to include these partitions in the RAID array.

Intel BIOS RAID

In Fedora 12, anaconda uses mdraid instead of dmraid to access Intel BIOS-RAID sets using the Intel Matrix Storage Manager metadata format. Mdraid supports Intel Matrix Storage Manager RAID 0, RAID 1, RAID 5, and RAID 10.

Care should be taken when upgrading previous versions of Fedora, as if the system contains Intel BIOS-RAID kits using the Intel Matrix Storage Manager metadata format, the device node names will change.

Fedora does not refer to these devices by default, but uses a UUID, so there should be no problem updating the standard installations of Fedora.

But if you are performing an installation that makes changes to local files /etc/fstab, /etc/crypttabor other configuration files that refer to device UUIDs, you may need to manually change the files that refer to devices by their UUIDs.

Create a software RAID partition

Select this option to add a software RAID partition. If the disk does not contain such partitions, this will be the only available choice.

Create RAID Device

Select this option to create a RAID device based on several existing software RAID partitions. This option will be available if at least two sections of software RAID are configured.

Clone a drive to create a RAID device

Select this option to configure a RAID mirror of an existing disk. This option is available when there are multiple disks in the system.

LVM: Allows you to create an LVM logical volume. The purpose of LVM (Logical Volume Manager) is a simple logical representation of physical storage, including hard drives. LVM manages individual physical disks or, to be more precise, their separate sections. Use LVM only if you are familiar with this technology.

To add one or more physical volumes to a group, first name the volume group, then select the volumes to add and, finally, configure the logical volumes in the groups using the Add, Modify and Delete options .

You can't remove the physical volume from the volume group. Take for example a 5 GB LVM physical volume partitions, which contains an 8 GB logical volume. Since it's not a problem, it's possible to use it. If you wish, you can then remove the physical volume from the volume group. In the example of reducing the physical volume.

LVM setting not available with text installation

The LVM setting is not available for text installation The installer allows you to change pre-configured LVM volumes. If you want to create a new LVM configuration, press Alt + F2 to open a terminal window and execute the command lvm. Press Alt + F1 to return to text mode.

Partition Table Columns

Above the partitioning table are labels representing the characteristics of the sections created. These designations are given below:

Device: This field displays the partition device device name.

Point mount / the RAID / the Volume: A the mount point is the location The Within the directory hierarchy AT which the exists a volume; the volume is "mounted" at this location. This field indicates where the partition is mounted. If there is a partition, there is no partition, Double-click on the edit button.

The Type: This field shows the partition's file system of the type (for example, an ext2, the ext3, the ext4, or a vfat).

Format: This column indicates whether the partition being created will be formatted.

Size (MB): This field shows the partition's size (in MB).

Start: This column indicates the cylinder from which the section starts.

End: This column indicates the cylinder with which the section ends.

Hide RAID devices / LVM group members: Select this check box to hide created RAID arrays or members of the LVM volume group.

Recommended partitioning scheme

X86 systems, AMD64 and Intel ® 64

If you don't have a good reason for splitting it in your own way, it is recommended to create the following partitions on x86, AMD64, and Intel 64 platforms:

Section swap

Section /boot

Section /

Swap partition (minimum 256 MB)

A swap partition is used to organize virtual memory. Data is placed in the swap section if the system does not have enough RAM to process it. Additionally, some power management features retain all memory contents in this section when the system goes into suspend mode.

If you are not sure what size of swap partition to choose, create it in size equal to twice the amount of RAM of your computer (but not more than 2 GB). It must be of type swap.

The following factors influence the allocation of appropriate space for the swap (in descending order):

Applications running on this system.

The amount of physical RAM.

The version of the operating system.

The size of the swap partition should be equal to twice the amount of RAM if the amount of RAM does not exceed 2 GB, the same amount of RAM for a memory of 2 GB or more, but not less than 32 MB.

Thus, if:

M = the amount of RAM in GB, and S = the volume of the swap partition in GB, then

If M <2

$\quad$ S = M * 2

Else

$\quad$ S = M + 2

Using this formula, you can easily determine that the swap area for a system with 2 GB of physical RAM is 4 GB, and for a 3 GB RAM, 5 GB. A large swap partition may make sense if you plan to increase the amount of RAM.

For systems with a significantly larger amount of RAM (more than 32 GB), it is quite possible to create a smaller swap partition (equal to the amount of RAM or even less).

Section /boot/(250 MB)

The section /boot/contains the kernel of the operating system (providing Fedora boot) and boot files. Due to certain limitations, you need to create an ext3 partition to store these files (usually 250 MB for the boot partition should be enough).

Btrfs

GRUB does not support the btrfs file system, so you cannot use it to organize a partition/boot.

Note

If your hard drive has more than 1024 cylinders (and your computer is over two years old), then you may have to create a partition /boot/if you want the rest of the disk space to occupy the root partition /.

Note

If you are using a RAID controller, please note that some BIOSes do not support booting from it. In such cases, the partition /boot/should be created in a partition that is not related to the RAID controller, for example, on a separate disk.

Section root(3.0-5.0 GB)

This is where " /" (the root directory) is located. In this setup, all files (except those stored in /boot) are on the root partition.

3 gigabytes is required for a minimal installation, and 5 gigabytes is enough for a full installation, including all package groups.

Root section and /root

The /(or root) partition is the directory structure. The /rootdirectory /root(sometimes pronounced "slash-root") is a directory.

There are many systems above. Choose partitions based on your particular system needs. For example, consider creating a separate /homepartition. Refer to Section "Recommendations for Creating Partitions" for more information.

If you create many partitions instead of one large /partition, upgrades become easier. Refer to Section, "Partition Screen" for more information.

The following table lists the minimum sizes for partitions containing specific directories. There is no need to create a separate section for these directories. For example, if a partition with a directory /foomust be at least 500 MB, and you decide not to create a separate partition /foo, then the size of the root partition /must be at least 500 MB.

Catalog	Minimum size
/	250 MB
/usr	250 MB, but do not place it in another section
/tmp	50 MB
/var	384 MB
/home	100 MB
/boot	250 MB

Leave the remaining space unallocated

Only assign storage requirements. You can allocate free space at any time. For more information, please refer to Appendix D, Introduction to LVM.

If you are not sure which partition structure is best to create, choose the standard option.

Recommendations for creating partitions

The optimal partitioning scheme is determined by how this particular Linux system will be used. The following are tips to help you more effectively allocate disk space.

If space will be used to store user data, create a separate partition for the directory in the volume group /home. If you upgrade or reinstall Fedora, those located in the /homefiles will not be lost.

Each kernel installed in the system will require approximately 10 MB in the partition /boot. The standard size of 250 MB is not enough only if you install a very large number of cores.

Btrfs

GRUB does not support the btrfs file system, so you cannot use it to organize a partition/boot.

The catalog /varcontains various applications, including the Apache web server. Package updates will be temporarily downloaded. Make sure that the partition containing the directory /varhas enough space, not only for hosting applications, but also for downloading the available updates.

Available updates

It can be available lately in a release cycle. You can add an update to it. Refer to Section "Installing from Additional Repositories" for more information.

The catalog /usrcontains the bulk of the Fedora software. To install a standard set of packages will require approximately 4 GB of space. Programmers who plan to use Fedora for software development are recommended to at least double this number.

Do not place /usrin a separate section

When placed /usrand /in different sections, the boot process will be much more complicated, and in some situations (for example, when installed on SCSI disks) the load will not be possible at all.

If possible, leave part of the LVM volume group space unallocated. This will allow adjusting to possible changes in the requirements of the space, and subsequently will not have to delete the data to free it.

Distributing the subdirectories between different sections will allow you to save their contents in case of reinstalling Fedora. For example, if the MySQL database is stored in /var/lib/mysql, you can put this directory in a separate partition, and then it will not need to be restored during reinstallation.

The following table contains an approximate partition structure for a system with one hard disk of 80 GB and 1 GB of RAM. Please note that approximately 10 GB of space is left unallocated.

Distribution example

This structure is not a universal solution.

Section	Size, type
/bo 6.21.4.1.1. Recommendations for creating partitions	250 MB, ext4
swap	2 GB, swap
physical volume LVM	Remaining space as LVM volume group

Table 6.4. Section structure example

The physical volume will be mapped to a standard volume group and divided into the following logical volumes:

Section	Size, type
/	13 GB, ext4
/var	4 GB, ext4
/home	50 GB, ext4

Table 6.5. Section structure example: LVM physical volume

Example 6.1. Section structure example

Adding sections

To add a new partition, select the New button. A dialog box appears (refer to "Creating a New Section").

Note

You must dedicate to this option. For more information, refer to Appendix A, Introduction to Disk Partitions.

Mount Point: Enter the partition's mount point. For example, if this partition should be the root partition, enter/; enter/bootfor the/bootpartition, and so on. You can also use the pull-down menu. The point is not to be set.

File System Type: for the partition. For more information on file system types, refer to Section "File System Types".

Allowable Drives: This field contains the hard disks installed on your system. If a hard disk is selected, then you can create a hard disk. The box is if not checked only, the partition will of the then by never the BE Created on That hard disk. Different using the checkbox Central by settings, you CAN have the anaconda PLACE partitions where clause you Up Need Them, or the let the anaconda Decide feature where clause partitions should! Go.

Size (MB): Enter the size of the partition in megabytes. Note that the default is 200 MB; if you do not change it, a partition of only 200 MB in size will be created.

The Additional Size the Options:-in Choose Whether to the keep the partition AT a fixed size bed, to the allow IT to "grow" (! Just fill up closeup the available hard drive space) to a certain point, or to the allow IT to grow to! Just fill the any remaining hard drive space available.

Having set the Fill all space up to (MB) parameter, you should also set the limit in the field to the right. This will allow you to leave some area of the disk free for future use.

This is the first part of the game. If unselected, a logical partition. Refer to Section "Sections within Sections - Overview of Additional Sections" , for more information.

OK: Agreeing with the specified parameters, to create a partition, click OK.

Cancel: Click Cancel if you do not want to create a partition.

File System Types

Fedora allows you to create different types of partitions depending on the file system used. Below is a brief description of the various file systems and examples of their use.

Btrfs - Btrfs is designed as a file system that can work with a large number of files, files and volumes larger than ext2, ext3 and ext4 file systems. Btrfs is designed to make the file system resilient to errors and to simplify the detection and correction of errors when they occur. It uses checksums to ensure the accuracy of data and metadata, and supports file system snapshots that can be used for backup or correction.

Because the installation program doesn't offer it by default. If you want to create a btrfs partition on the drive, you must commence the instalation process with the boot option icantbelieveitsnotbtr. Refer to Download Options for instructions.

Btrfs is still experimental.

Fedora 12 has Btrfs for preview, to give you the opportunity to experiment w th this file system. You should not choose Btrfs for partitions that will contain valuable data or that are essential for the operation of important systems.

ext2 - The ext2 file system supports standard Unix file types (regular files, directories, symbolic links, etc.). The allowed length of file names is 255 characters.

ext3 is based on the ext2 file system and its main advantage over ext2 is the ability to journal. Logging reduces file system recovery time after a crash, since there is no need to perform a checkfsck [3] .

ext4 - The ext4 file system is based on the ext3 file system and has a number of improvements. These improvements include support for file systems and larger files, faster and more efficient allocation of disk space, an unlimited number of subdirectories in one directory, faster file system checks, as well as more reliable journaling. The ext4 file system is selected by default and is highly recommended for use.

physical volume (LVM) - By creating one or more physical volume sections (LVM), you can create an LVM logical volume. LVM can improve performance when using hard drives.

Software RAID - Creating two or more RAID partitions allows you to create software RAID devices.

swap - Swap partitions are used to support virtual memory. In other words, the data falls into the swap partition when the system does not have enough RAM to process the data.

vfat is a FAT-compatible Linux file system that supports long Microsoft Windows file names. Itanium computers in the partition/boot/efi/should use this file system.

Change sections

To edit a section, click the Edit button or double-click an existing section.

Note

You can only change the partition's mount point. You need to make it.

Deleting a section

To delete a partition, select it in the Sections table and click the Delete button. Confirm the deletion in response to the prompt.

Further installation instructions for for x86, AMD64, and the Intel ® 64 systems, skip to Section "Setting the boot oader for x86, AMD64 and the Intel ® 64" .

Save changes to disk

The installation program will ask you to confirm the selected partitioning settings. Click Save Changes to Disk to continue the installation.

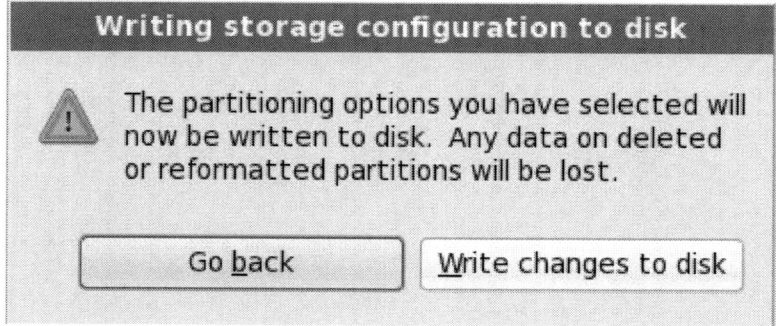

Write storage information to disk

If you are sure that everything is selected correctly, click Save Changes to Disk.

Last chance safe cancellation

Up to this point during the installation, the installer has not saved any changes on your computer. When you click Save Changes to Disk, the installer will allocate space on your hard disk and begin installing Fedora. Depending on the partitioning scheme chosen, this process may include deleting existing data.

To review your chosen settings, click Return. To interrupt the installation, turn off the computer. To do this, press the power button on the system unit and hold it pressed for a few seconds.

After you click Write changes to disk, you will not be able to cancel the installation. If the installation was interrupted (for example, the computer was turned off), you will not be able to use your computer until you restart and complete the installation process or until you install another OS.

Boot Loader Configuration for x86, AMD64 and Intel 64

To start a computer without a bootable floppy disk, you usually need to install a bootloader. The loader is the first program that runs when the computer starts up and is responsible for loading and transferring control to the operating system kernel. The kernel, in turn, initializes the rest of the operating system.

Installing in text mode

When installing in text mode, the bootloader will be automatically configured and its settings cannot be changed during the installation process.

GRUB (GRand Unified Bootloader), installed by default, is a powerful boot loader. GRUB can load various open operating systems as well as systems owned by commercial companies with chain loading (the mechanism for loading unsupported operating systems, for example, DOS or Windows, with the help of another bootloader).

GRUB menu

By default, the GRUB menu will not be displayed. The exceptions are dual-boot systems. To show the GRUB menu at boot time, before loading the kernel, press and hold the Shift key.

There are no If other operating systems on your computer, or you are completely removing any other operating systems the installation program will install GRUB as your boot loader without any intervention. In that case you may continue on to Section - the Package Group is the Selection.

The system may already have a boot loader installed. If your boot loader does not recognize Linux partitions, there may be problems booting Fedora. We recommend using the GRUB boot loader for booting Linux and most other operating systems. Installation instructions are provided in this chapter.

Installing GRUB

When installing GRUB, it can overwrite an existing bootloader.

The installation program will install GRUB into the master boot record (MBR) of the device hosting the root file system. To cancel the installation of a new bootloader, deselect Install bootloader in / dev / sda.

Warning

If for some reason you decide not to install GRUB, you will not be able to boot the system directly, and you will have to use a different boot method (for example, a commercial bootloader). Use this option only if you definitely have another way to boot the computer!

If other operating systems are installed on your computer, Fedora will try to automatically detect them and configure GRUB to load them. You can do this yourself if GRUB does not detect the system.

To add, remove or change the detected operating systems, use the appropriate options.

To add

Select Add to add another operating system to GRUB.

Select a disk partition containing the boot OS from the list and give it a name. GRUB will show it in the boot menu.

Edit

To change an entry in the GRUB menu, select it and click the Edit button.

Delete

To delete an entry from the GRUB menu, select the entry and click the Delete button.

Select the Default checkbox in the preferred section row to select the system to load by default. If you do not select the default boot image, you will not be able to continue the installation.

Note

The names listed in the Label column will be entered at the boot prompt with a text interface to load the desired operating system.

In the GRUB bootloader window, you can select the desired label using the arrow keys or change it by pressing the e key. You will see a list of configuration file options for the selected system.

The use of loader passwords provides an additional level of protection where physical access to your server is possible.

If you installed a bootloader, you must determine the password to protect your system. If the bootloader password is not set, users who have access to your computer can transfer parameters to the kernel and crack the protection. If the bootloader password is set, you will need to enter the password first to configure the bootloader settings. But if someone has physical access to the computer, then it is possible to load it from a floppy disk, a CD or a USB device, provided the BIOS is supported. The system safety plan should also consider alternative boot methods.

GRUB Passwords Not Required

If you are a physician, you must not have a GRUB password if you need to use it. HOWEVER, the if an untrusted name person the get CAN Physical access to your computer's keyboard and monitor, That name person CAN reboot the the system and access the GRUB . A password is helpful in this case.

If you decide to use a bootloader password to enhance system security, check the Set bootloader password box.

Then enter the password and confirm it.

The GRUB stores the password in encrypted The form, SO IT CAN not the BE or the read Recovered. You forget the If boot password, boot the system normally and then change the password entry in the/boot/grub/grub.conffile. If you can't boot up, you must be able to reset the GRUB password.

If there is no need to change the GRUB password, use the utility grub-md5-crypt. For more information, see the help page man grub-md5-crypt.

GRUB recognizes only the QWERTY layout.

When choosing a GRUB password, please note that GRUB recognizes only the QWERTY layout, regardless of the keyboard connected. If you use a keyboard whose layout is significantly different, remember the key order, not the password word itself.

To configure additional bootloader parameters, for example, change the order of devices or pass parameters to the kernel, check the Configure advanced bootloader parameters box and click the continue button.

Advanced bootloader configuration

Now that you have selected the installable bootloader, you can determine where to install it. You can install the bootloader in one of two places:

The master boot record (MBR) is where the boot loader is installed, unless it already has another operating system loader, such as System Commander. If you're trying to find out how to boot, you'll be able to control the system. If you install it in the MBR, for your machine boots, GRUB presents a boot prompt. You can boot the boot loader to boot.

The first sector of the boot partition is recommended if another boot loader is already installed. In this case, first, this loader will get control. Then you can configure it to start GRUB, which in turn will load Fedora.

GRUB as a secondary bootloader

If GRUB is installed as a secondary boot loader, you will need to change the settings of the main boot loader when the kernel changes. On dual boot systems, it is recommended to use GRUB as the main boot loader.

Note

If you are using a RAID adapter, please note that not all BIOSes support booting from RAID adapter disks. In such cases, do not install the boot loader in the MBR of the RAID array. The loader must be installed in the MBR on the disk where the partition is located /boot/.

If you will be using only Fedora, select the MBR.

Click the Change Disk Order button if you are not satisfied with the disk order or the disks are confused in the BIOS. Changing the drive order can be useful if there are several SCSI adapters or both SCSI and IDE adapters, and you, in turn, want to boot from a SCSI device.

Note

When creating partitions on your hard drive, please note that the BIOS of some older computers can access only the first 1024 cylinders of the disk. In this case, to boot Linux, allocate /bootenough space for the partition within the first 1024 disk cylinders. Other Linux sections may be located behind the 1024 cylinder.

In the program parted1024 cylinders are equal to 528 MB. For more information, contact:

http://www.pcguide.com/ref/hdd/bios/sizeMB504-c.html

Rescue mode

Rescue mode provides a system for your hard drive. If you are unable to get it, it will be running. Using rescue mode, you can access the files stored on your system's hard drive, even if you can't actually run Fedora from that hard drive. If you need to use rescue mode, try the following method:

An the x86 the Boot, on AMD64 machines, or the Intel ® 64 from the any installation system medium, such as with the the CD, a DVD, the USB, or the PXE, and of the type linux rescueAT the installation not boot the prompt. Refer to Chapter 16, Basic System Recovery for a more complete description of rescue mode.

Alternative system loaders

Fedora uses the GRUB boot loader by default, but this does not exclude the possibility of using other boot loaders. For example, you can select LILO, SYSLINUX, Acronis Disk Director Suite, Apple Boot Camp bootloader.

Package Group Selection

Having determined most of the installation options, you can choose which packages to install.

First, a package selection dialog appears, describing the default package set on Fedora. This dialog may look different depending on the version of Fedora you are installing.

Installing from a Live Image

When you install a system from a Fedora Live image, the selection of packages for installation will not be available. The reason is that the image of the installed system is copied, rather than installing packages from the repository. To select specific packages after installation, use the program to add and remove software.

Installing in text mode

When installing Fedora in text mode, the selection of packages for installation will not be available. The installer will automatically select from the main group the packages necessary for the system to work after the installation process is completed and it is ready to install new packages and updates. After the installation is completed, you can change the set of packages using the special application for adding and removing programs.

By default, Fedora installs applications suitable for home computers. To add or remove an application, select the corresponding option from the list:

Office applications

In this menu, you can choose to install OpenOffice.org, a project planning program, image editing programs (such as GIMP), and multimedia applications.

Software development

This group includes all the necessary tools for creating software in Fedora.

Web server

This option allows you to install an Apache web server.

If you choose to accept the current package list, skip ahead to Section "Installing Packages."

To select a component, click on the checkbox beside it (refer to Figure 6.29, "Package Group Selection").

To change the standard set of packages, select the Refine Software Selection check box. Click Next to go to the package group selection window.

Installing from additional repositories

You can specify additional package repositories. The repository is a place in the network where software packages with metadata describing them are stored. Very rarely, packages can be installed on their own - most Fedora packages require the installation of other packages.

The installer uses metadata to check and install package dependencies.

Main settings:

The installation repository will be automatically selected. It includes software for the installation CD / DVD.

Fedora 12 - i386 contains the complete collection of Fedora 12 programs plus stable versions of additional programs. When installing Fedora 12 from a set of CDs or DVDs, this option will not offer additional features, but when installing from a LiveCD you will have access to a wide range of packages. To do this, the computer must have access to the Internet.

The Fedora 12 - i386 - Updates repository contains a complete collection of Fedora 12 packages plus stable versions of additional programs. This option not only installs the selected software, but also guarantees the availability of the latest versions. To do this, the computer must have access to the Internet.

To enable packages from other repositories, select Add additional repositories. After that you can specify the location of the repository of interest. Depending on its settings, it will be possible to install not only Fedora packages.

To change the repository location, select it from the list and click the Edit repository button.

Network access required

If you change the repository data during a local installation, for example, when installing from a Fedora DVD, the installer will request network configuration information.

If you select Add additional repositories, the Edit Repository window appears. Enter his name and link.

Fedora Mirror Servers

To find a Fedora software mirror for you, refer to http://fedoraproject.org/wiki/Mirrors.

Located you have once recording a by mirror, to the Determine the the URL to use, the find the directory on the by mirror that contains a directory named is repodata. For instance, the "Everything" repository for Fedora is typically located in a directory tree, where is a system architecture name. releases/12/Everything/arch/osarch

Once you provide information on the installation metadata over the network. Software package selection system. See Section- Selecting Installable Software" for more information on selecting packages.

Repository metadata will be deleted upon return

Pressing the Back button in the package selection window will delete the settings of additional repositories. There is currently no function to delete a separate repository.

Choice of software to install

To refine the list of packages to install, select Configure now. A window will open where you can add or remove packages from the list. When finished, click the continue button.

Install Language Support

Select Customize now for install support for additional languages. Refer to Section - "Support for Additional Languages" for more information on configuring language support.

Package installation

All the packages have been installed. Your computer's speed.

While recording the selected packages, Fedora reports on the installation progress on the screen. In the case of installation from a CD, a disk change request will periodically appear. After inserting the next disk, click OK to continue the installation.

For your reference, /root/install.logyou can find your system.

After the installation is complete, select Restart. You can remove the disc from the CD-ROM before rebooting.

Installing from a Live Image

When you install from a Fedora Live image, the restart prompt does not appear. You can continue to work in the Live environment and reboot the system at any time.

Installation completion

Congratulations! The installation of Fedora is complete!

The installation program will offer to prepare the system for a reboot. Remember to remove all installation media if they were not automatically removed during the reboot.

[2] The root password is the administrative password for your Fedora system. You must be logged in as root for system maintenance only. The root account is not subject to any restrictions affecting ordinary users, so changes made by root can affect the operation of the entire system.

[3] The program is fsckused to check the integrity of the metadata in the file system and to restore one or more Linux file systems.

Troubleshooting Installation on systems in the Intel ® and AMD

Unable to Download Fedora

Unable to boot from a RAID controller?

If you completed the installation and after that you cannot boot the system, you may have to reinstall the system, breaking the disk into sections differently.

Some BIOSes do not support booting from RAID controllers. After installation, it is possible that a bootloader prompt (for example GRUB:) and a blinking cursor will appear on the text screen . In this case, you will need to repartition the drives in your system.

Both with manual and automatic disk partitioning, you will need to create a partition /bootoutside the RAID array, for example, on a separate hard disk. If the described problems occur with RAID controllers, you must use an internal hard disk.

You must also install your preferred boot loader (GRUB or LILO) in the MBR disk outside of the RAID array. The loader should be installed on the same disk as the partition /boot/.

After completing these changes, you will be able to complete the installation and correctly boot the system.

Does the system generate Signal 11 errors?

The "signal 11" error, often referred to as a segmentation failure, means that the program is accessing an unknown area of memory. If during the installation an error "signal 11" is received, most likely, this is due to the error code of the installed programs or hardware failure.

If you receive an error signal during your installation, it will Like other operating systems, hardware. Hardware may not be able to meet any other demands, even if they work properly under another OS.

Ensure that you have the latest installer updates and nstallation images. If you are unable to boot from the atest disk images, your hardware may be causing the problem. Most often, these are defects in the RAM or processor cache. You can try to correct this error by disabling the processor cache in the BIOS. You can also swap memory modules to other slots to determine if the problem is with memory or slots.

In addition, check the installation CDs. Anaconda has the ability to verify the integrity of the media. This can be done when installing from a CD, DVD or ISO image located on a hard disk or on a network. Red Hat recommends that you check all media before the installation process and don't rush to report errors (most of the errors are actually related to incorrectly written CDs). To validate, type in the invitationboot:

linux mediacheck

For more information about signal 11 errors, refer to:

http://www.bitwizard.nl/sig11/

Problems running the installation

Problems running the graphical installation

Some video cards may encounter problems when running the graphical installer mode. If the installation program cannot be started with the standard settings, the screen resolution will be reduced. If this fails, the installation program will run in text mode.

One possible solution during the installation. If you choose the boot menu, you can use this xdriver=vesaoption. Alternatively, the resolution=boot option can be used. This option may be most helpful for laptop users. It driver=should be noted that the driver should not be loaded for your video card. If this works, you should be unable to detect your video card automatically. Refer to Chapter 8, Boot Options for more information on boot options.

Note

To disable support for the frame buffer and allow the installer to run in text mode, pass a parameter during the boot process nofb. This may be necessary if screen readers are used.

Problems during installation

Mistake: No Fedora Installer Found

If you receive an error message stating that the device is not found suitable for installing the FedoraSCSI controller.

You can also refer to the hardware compatibility list on LinuxQuestions.org:

http://www.linuxquestions.org/hcl/index.php

Save debug messages without removable media

If you're looking for an error

Debugging

Will show detailed information about the error.

Save

stores error information locally or remotely.

Output

closes the window.

You the select the if the Save from the main dialog, you CAN from list choose from the the following options:

Save locally

saves the error information on the local hard disk.

Save remotely

stores error information on a remote resource using the SCP command .

Save to Bugzilla

Red Hat buggy tracking system, Bugzilla. Description of the bug.

Problems with partition tables

If you receive an installation process (Section - "Initializing a Hard Disk") that says something similar to:

Error processing drive sda. Maybe it needs to be reinitialized. YOU WILL LOSE ALL DATA ON THIS DRIVE!

You may not have to be able to use your computer.

Similar problems arise for users of EZ-BIOS and similar programs and may lead to data loss (unless you back them up before the installation begins).

If you're not doing so, you should always be made.

Using unallocated space

If you created partitions swap,/ (the root) and you want the root partition to the unallocated space on the disk, it can, nevertheless, does not fill the hard drive.

f your disk has more than 1024 cylinders, you must create a partition /bootin order for the root partition to occupy all the free space on the disk.

Other problems with partitioning

If you create partitions manually and cannot proceed to the next screen, it is possible that you did not create all the partitions necessary to continue the installation.

At a minimum, you will need to create the following sections:

Root partition /

A partition /bootwith a file system type that GRUB can read (for example, ext4) if /btrfs is selected for the partition.

A <swap> partition of type swap

Note

When defining a partition point Anaconda automatically assigns the mount point for you.

Are there any Python program errors?

Sometimes when upgrading or installing Fedora, the anaconda installer may fail to exit and display Python errors or debug messages. This happens after selecting individual packages or when trying to save the update protocol to a directory /tmp/and looks like this:

Traceback (innermost last):

File   "/var/tmp/anaconda-7.1usr/lib/anaconda/iw/progress_gui.py", line 20, in run

rc = self.todo.doInstall ()

File   "/var/tmp/anaconda-7.1usr/lib/anaconda/todo.py", line 1468, in doInstall

self.fstab.savePartitions ()

File "fstab.py", line 221, in savePartitions

sys.exit (0)

SystemExit: 0

Local variables in innermost frame:

self: <fstab.GuiFstab instance at 8446fe0>

sys: <module 'sys' (built-in)>

ToDo object: (itodo ToDc p1 (dp2 S'method 'p3 (iimage CdromInstallMethod

p4 (dp5 S'progressWindow 'p6 <failed>

This error occurs in some cases when links to /tmp/are symbolic links to other directories or have been changed after creation. Such links in the installation process do not work, as a result, the installation program cannot record information and fails.

If you encounter this situation, first try to get the latest Anaconda program updates, which, together with the relevant instructions, can be found at:

http://fedoraproject.org/wiki/Anaconda/Updates

Anaconda site may also be useful:

http://fedoraproject.org/wiki/Anaconda

You can also search for bug reports. To search Red Hat's bug tracking system, go to:

http://bugzilla.redhat.com/bugzilla/

Problems after installation

Problem with grub graphic screen on x86?

If for some reason you need to disable the graphical boot screen, you can do it as root by editing the file /boot/grub/grub.confand rebooting the system.

To do this, comment out the line that starts with the word splashimagein the file grub.conf, adding the symbol to the beginning of the line#.

Press Enter to exit edit mode.

Return to the GRUB screen and click bto boot the system with the new parameters.

After rebooting, the file grub.confwill be downloaded again, and the changes will take effect.

You can return the graphical loading screen by removing the comment or re-adding the above line to the file grub.conf.

Download in graphical environment

If you have installed the X Window System, a graphical desktop environment but after logging in does not appear, you can start the X Window graphical interface using the command startx.

As soon as you enter this command and press Enter, the graphical desktop environment will appear.

However, this will solve the problem only once and will not affect subsequent registrations in the system.

To configure the system authorization in graphical mode, edit the file /etc/inittabby changing only one number in the runlevel section. Then restart the computer. The next registration in the system will be in graphical mode.

Go to the shell prompt. If you are working as a regular user, use the command suto switch to root mode.

Then type the command gedit /etc/inittabto edit the desired file in the gedit editor. The file /etc/inittabwill be open for editing. You will see a file fragment similar to the following:

Default runlevel. The runlevels used are:

0 - halt (Do NOT set initdefault to this)

1 - Single user mode

2 - Multiuser, without NFS (The same as 3, if not have networking)

3 - Full multiuser mode

4 - unused

5 - X11

6 - reboot (Do NOT set initdefault to this)

id: 3: initdefault:

To change the registration window from console mode to graphical, change the number in the line id:3:initdefault:from 3to 5.

Warning

Change only the default run level number from 3to 5.

The modified line should look like this:

  id:5:initdefault:

Then save the file and exit the editor by pressing the Ctrl + the Q. A message will appear indicating that the file has been modified, as well as a suggestion to save these changes. Click Save to save.

Thus, your next registration will be in graphical mode.

Problems with the X Window System (GUI)

If you cannot start X (the X Window System), you may not have installed it during the initial installation.

If you need an X system, you can either install the packages from the Fedora installation media or upgrade.

If you decide to upgrade, choosing the packages to be nstalled during the upgrade, check the X Window System and the GNOME, KDE, or both.

Refer to Section - "Switching to the Graphical Authorization Mode" for more detail on the desktop environment.

Server X crashes for non-root users

If server X fails every time a non-super-user (root) logs in, it is possible that the file system is full (or there is simply not enough disk space).

To verify the cause of this problem, run the following command:

df -h

The team dfwill help determine which section is full. For more information about the command dfand its parameters (for example, -hmentioned in the example), refer to the help page dfby typing man dfin the prompt.

If the section is more than 90% full, you should pay attention to it. Sections /home/and /tmp/can quickly be filled with user files. It is possible to partially free up space by deleting old files. After that, you can try to run X again.

Login Issues

If you did not create a user account during the firstboot process, open a console window by pressing Ctrl + Alt + F2, and log in as root.

If you don't remember the root password, boot the system in exclusive mode (linux single).

If you are using an x86 computer and GRUB is installed as a bootloader, on the GRUB screen, click eto edit the boot options. You will see a list of configuration file options for your chosen system.

Select the line that starts with kernel, and click eto edit it.

Add at the end of the line kernel:

single

Press Enter to exit edit mode.

Once the boot loader screen has been returned, it has been returned bto the system.

After booting in exclusive mode and accessing the prompt #, enter passwd rootto set a new root user password. Then enter the command shutdown -r nowto restart the system with a new password.

If you can't remember your user account password, you must become root. To become root, type su -and enter your password password when prompted. Then, type passwd <username>. This allows you to enter a password for the user account.

If the graphical login screen does not appear, check if your hardware is compatible. A list of compatible hardware can be found on the linuxquestions.org website.

http://www.linuxquestions.org/hcl/index.php

RAM is defined incorrectly.

Sometimes the kernel incorrectly determines the total amount of installed RAM. You can verify this by running the command cat /proc/meminfo.

Find out if the displayed size matches the amount of RAM installed on your system. If they are not equal, add the /boot/grub/grub.confline to the file:

mem=xxM

Replace the xxsize of the installed RAM in megabytes.

The file /boot/grub/grub.confin the example described above will look like this:

NOTICE: You have a / boot partition. This means that

all kernel paths are relative to / boot /

default = 0

timeout = 30

splashimage = (hd0,0) /grub/splash.xpm.gz

 title Fedora (2.6.27.19-170.2.35.fc10.i686)

root (hd0,1)

kernel /vmlinuz-2.6.27.19-170.2.35.fc10.i686 ro root = UUID = 04a07c13-e6bf-6d5a-b207-002689545705 mem = 1024M

initrd /initrd-2.6.27.19-170.2.35.fc10.i686.img

Immediately after the reboot, the changes made to grub.confwill take effect.

Once on the GRUB bootloader screen, enter for editing e. You will see a list of configuration file options for your chosen system.

Select the line that starts with kernel, and click eto edit it.

At the end of the line, kerneladd

mem=xxM

where xxdenotes the amount of RAM your system.

Press Enter to exit edit mode.

Once the boot loader screen has been returned, it has been returned bto the system.

Itanium computer users will need to add elilobefore the download commands.

Do not forget to replace the xxsize of RAM. To download, press Enter.

Printer does not work

If you do not know how to set up the printer, or can't set it up correctly, try using the Printer Settings Utility.

Run the command at the shell prompt redhat-config-printerto start the printer setup utility. If you are not a root user, you will be prompted to enter the root password to continue.

When starting service hangs httpdor sendmail

If the service httpd(based on Apache) or Sendmail hangs on startup, check the file for the /etc/hostsfollowing line:

localhost.localdomain localhost

Part III. Advanced installation options

This part of the tutorial covers more complex aspects of installing Fedora, including:

Boot options;

Installation without carriers;

Installation using vnc;

Automation of the installation process.

Installation and installation options for administrators. To use the boot options, type in the prompt. linux boot parameter:

If you use multiple boot options, separate them with a space. For example:

linux option1 option2 option3

Anaconda boot options

The most ankonda installer has many boot options, most are listed on the wiki http://fedoraproject.org/wiki/Anaconda/Options.

Kernel boot options

The http://fedoraproject.org/wiki/KernelCommonProblems page lists many common kernel boot options. / Usr / share / doc / kernel-doc- version/Documentation/kernel-parameters.txt, which is installed with the kernel-doc package.

Rescue mode

The Fedora installation and of The rescue at discs may not boot with an either rescue at mode, or the load the installation system. For more information on rescue discs, refer to Section - "Booting the Computer in Rescue Mode" .

Setup installation system in the boot menu

In the download menu, you can specify some installation options, including:

Language

Screen resolution

Interface type

Installation method

Network settings

Language definition

To set the language for both the installation process and the target system, specify its ISO code using the parameter lang. Use the option keymapto customize the keyboard layout.

For example, ISO codes el_GRand grdenote the Greek language and the Greek keyboard layout:

linux lang=el_GR keymap=gr

Interface Setup

The screen resolution is (640x480) with the parameter lowres. To use a specific screen resolution, enter as a boot parameter. For example, for a screen resolution of 1024x768, enter: resolution = value

linux resolution=1024x768

To run the installation process in text mode, enter:

linux text

To enable support for a serial console, enter serialas an additional option.

Use to allow redirection to a remote screen. In this command, replace the IP address of the system with the remote display. display=ip:0ip

The screen resolution is (640x480) with the parameter owres. To use a specific screen resolution, enter as a boot parameter. For example, for a screen resolution of 1024x768, enter: resolution = value

Anaconda Update

To install Fedora, you can use the new version of the anaconda installer, perhaps a newer version compared to the version on your installation media.

Boot option

linux updates

will show the prompt in which the floppy is requested with anaconda updates . You do not need to set this parameter if you are installing over the network and have already placed the contents of the image with the updates in rhupdates/on the server.

To download anaconda updates from the network, use:

  linux updates=

then specifying the URL of the location where the updates are located.

Choosing an installation method

Use the option askmethodto display additional menus that allow you to specify the installation method and network settings. You can also customize the installation method and network settings in the prompt itself boot:.

The Specify the installation To method from the boot:the prompt, use the repooption. Refer to -"Installation Methods" for the supported installation methods.

Installation method	Parameter format
CD or DVD drive	repo=cdrom:device
Hard drive	repo=hd:device/path
HTTP server	repo=http://host/path
FTP server	repo=ftp://username:password@host/path
NFS server	repo=nfs:server:/path
ISO images on the NFS server	repo=nfsiso:server:/path

350

Conclusion

If you are new to the Python programming language, it is better to learn Python3. But if you are learning the Python programming language to work on a particular project, which version you need to learn depends on the state of the auxiliary modules you will use in the project. Not all Python modules/programs on the market have been imported into Python3 yet.

If the auxiliary modules you plan to use in your project have already been imported into Python3, you can learn Python3. However, if these modules have not yet been released in Python3, you may wish to continue with Python2. But in any case, keep in mind that Python3 is the future of this language and that one day Python2 will be entirely out of circulation.

47213160R00199

Made in the USA
San Bernardino, CA
11 August 2019